DARE TO DREAM

DARE TO DREAM

LORRAINE LEWIS

Matador
Unit E2 Airfield Business Park,
Harrison Road, Market Harborough,
Leicestershire. LE16 7UL
Tel: 0116 2792299
Email: books@troubador.co.uk
Web: www.troubador.co.uk/matador
Twitter: @matadorbooks

ISBN 978 1803130 897

British Library Cataloguing in Publication Data.
A catalogue record for this book is available from the British Library.

Printed and bound in Great Britain by 4edge Limited
Typeset in 11pt Minion Pro by Troubador Publishing Ltd, Leicester, UK

Matador is an imprint of Troubador Publishing Ltd

To Mum, Dad and Lee. Thank you for always inspiring me, giving me strength and believing in me. With you all in my life anything is possible.

PROLOGUE

I've always wanted to write a book, ever since I was a child. I loved reading and writing; however, I couldn't think of anything to write about that would have some meaning, purpose or be something that people would find interesting enough to read.

This meant that I'd push this idea of writing a book to the back of my mind, even if now and again the thought of it did bubble to the surface.

I happily worked my way through life, ticking items off my vision board that I created when I was twelve. Whilst it was great to do this, by the time I was twenty-five, I had ticked everything on it off – I had become a barrister; I had bought the house I wanted; I had travelled; I'd got the car I wanted; and I had bought all the things I had ever wanted. Whilst I should have been buzzing, I now felt totally flat – what next? Surely, I should feel more fulfilled than this. When I would share this with people, they didn't get it. What more could you want, when you had everything you wanted?

I didn't want to be defined based on my career choice, the fact I liked to party, I was the person always going on holiday or I always had nice bags and shoes. If I died tomorrow, I really didn't want those to be the things people remembered me by. So, I continued with daily life, thinking this must be it.

Then, following my mother-in-law's diagnosis of cancer in 2010, and everything that flowed from that diagnosis, everything changed for me. It changed the way I looked at life, the way I thought about life and what I in fact wanted to do with my life. For someone who had never really experienced or been surrounded by death, it was an eye-opener and a game changer. When you're thrown into a world where there is a delicate balance between life and death and where your life can change in an instant, it makes you wake up and think about your own.

If that hadn't happened, would I have discovered who I really am, the things that really matter to me or the things I really love doing? I don't know. However, what I do know is it opened my eyes in a way that I never ever imagined.

If anyone had said to me or my husband Lee in 2010 that eleven years later, we'd be running a growing charity that was doing well, we would have laughed in their faces.

Before the Lewis Foundation, we had no interest in charities or contributing to charities. No one we really knew did either. I think that's because for me, none of them had really communicated with me in a way that drew me in; I couldn't find a connection with what they were trying to achieve. It wasn't something I gave much thought to other than when I had to give money to sponsor someone. Even then, I wasn't really interested in the cause.

However, in those years that I spent in the hospital – watching and observing others, whilst experiencing my own grief and challenges, seeing acts of kindness in the purest form – I felt I had to do something. At the time we were going through the journey, I couldn't do it, but when we came out the other side, I was a different person, and I knew what I needed to do. I felt stupid raising it with my husband Lee at first – what if he just wanted to put the whole thing behind him? We had suffered enough, but he was feeling what I was too. We wanted to do something to change the world together.

We had this idea of giving people gifts to cheer them up and make them smile. We knew this was going to make a difference; we couldn't see what the end of this vision would look like, but we were going to give it a go and make it a reality. Hopefully, it would help some people in the process.

When we decided we were going to set up a charity giving gifts for free to cancer patients, most people we know thought we were crazy. We didn't listen as we believed so much that this was going to help people in their time of need, even if, initially, no one else saw how it would help.

I'm so glad we didn't get dissuaded when people didn't get it, didn't know who we were and didn't support us, who thought we were dodgy as we tried to convince them that we really didn't want anything in return for what we were doing.

It taught me that against all my beliefs, we can live in a society where people can genuinely care for one another even though they're strangers. That they have each other's back, that no one is alone.

Flowing from this, I finally discovered what I was meant to do with my life, which was to help support others and, via The Lewis Foundation, I continue to do this every day and hopefully inspire others in the process.

PART 1

1996

I always knew I wanted to become a barrister from as young as I can remember. I was aware of what the profession was because I remember watching those daytime law shows at home with my mum. My dad was at work. My mum didn't work as she gave it up to look after me and my brother, to bring us up. My mum and I would always watch our favourite, which was *LA Law*. We would spend the episode problem-solving, shouting at the TV and cheering when a conviction was secured. My mum was a firm believer in justice, which was why she was so passionate and fired-up watching it.

For that reason, I always knew I wanted to prosecute and wanted to work for an organisation where I could prosecute. It was a dream, but it was something I knew that I wanted. I had no idea how I was going to get there or even if I could get there. We knew no one who did law or had even been to university. On paper, my chances were slim and could have easily been argued as non-existent if you went by what society defined a barrister to be like.

I was from a working-class family, lived on a council estate and went to a state school. I knew I had a brain, and I was pretty good at school, so academic-wise I could achieve what I needed to. So, I had no doubt that was what I was going to do when I grew up. It was just whether life would let me.

I was a child that was super quiet and worked really hard. You would find me reading all the time, and I lived in the library. My parents would take me and my brother every Friday after school when my dad finished work so that I could top up on new books. I loved the library (dream job number two if finances allowed it).

For me, it wasn't about being popular at school. I had friends and no issue. No one gave me a hard time for wanting to learn or do well. I just looked forward to the time when I could leave and get on with the future life I wanted to lead.

My school wasn't the best school in the world. It didn't have the best reputation, but that didn't dampen what I wanted to achieve when I grew up. My self-belief and ambition from an early age was really strong. This was due to the beliefs my parents had instilled in me that I could do and be whoever I wanted to be. They didn't have a choice as to what they would do when they were older. As soon as school was over for them, it was time for them both to head to the world of work to help pay the bills and support the family. They wanted to ensure that if there was something my brother and I wanted to do, we didn't miss out like they had.

The only people that dampened my beliefs were the very people that were supposed to guide me and support me in my learning environment. Those were teachers, the ones who were supposed to inspire and encourage you. That's what I thought until I had my first experience of negativity when I had a 'career chat' aged twelve years old. This was a time when the schools were starting the conversation: 'what do you want to do when you leave school?' I think a lot of people at that age don't take it very seriously. Often, people don't know what they want to do next week, let alone in four years' time when they leave school. I don't think the teachers were expecting anyone with any real career aspirations to come in.

I remember feeling quite proud and satisfied that I knew. I had a list of questions mentally prepared that I needed to ask as I had never had an opportunity to ask someone before how I could become a barrister.

I hoped they would be impressed but, more importantly, I needed them to help me and guide me to get to where I wanted to be. I went in and she asked me what I wanted to be. I told her I wanted to be a barrister. I was sitting there expectantly, waiting for some praise, some suggestion and guidance on the route how to get there. All I got was a look that said, *come on now, don't be ridiculous.* Followed by the words, "Well, that won't happen because you're a woman and you're black."

I was taken aback and didn't know what to say. I had never before encountered anyone saying my skin colour or gender meant that I was less likely to achieve what I wanted.

It was a thought that hadn't even entered my head.

After that, it was silent. I said nothing; she said nothing. We just looked at each other. Did she think it was a joke? Was she waiting for me to backtrack? I wasn't sure. I knew I couldn't speak because I was scared if I did, I would be angry, and then I would get in trouble for shouting at the teacher. It was the angry feeling that caused tears to come, and I also didn't want to cry. I said nothing, which meant that I wouldn't give away how upset I was. I felt humiliated and stupid.

Instead, I was guided to something completely different. "An office administrator – that would be good for you. We could get you some work experience in a year or two at the local council." Whilst she babbled on about what that would entail, I didn't hear a word of it. I just looked at her mouth moving, and I didn't hear a thing.

I was sent on my way with a printout for a job that I had never said I wanted to do. There was no further mention or discussion regarding me becoming a barrister. It was as if I had never mentioned it. I didn't know what to do. Did I accept what she said and give up now to save wasting my time?

I couldn't understand why it was so hard to find a positive, encouraging environment. It was like society had a certain view of who I was and where I should be, so I should stay in my lane. If I tried to take a step out of it, I was put back and reminded that I needed to get back where I should be.

I remember going home to my parents with my piece of paper. I told them what had happened. They didn't insult the teacher; they just told me what they always had. I could do or be whatever I wanted to be. Nothing was going to change that, and someone's words shouldn't change that either. I was determined that I would push past the boundaries that were being placed around me. Between myself and my parents, we would figure out a way.

I decided I knew what I wanted; I was going to get it; and no one was going to stop me.

1998

My life was pretty much what a normal fourteen-year-old's life would be. I went to school, I spent a lot of time in the library (in and out of school), hung out with friends and was at home with my mum, dad and brother. Pretty standard really and not very exciting.

However, not long after my fourteenth birthday, I slowly noticed I started to feel ill any time I ate anything. Literally anything. Something didn't feel right when I ate. I would eat certain things and it would be so painful, like torture, and I felt unwell all the time. The best way to describe it would be like razor blades shredding the inside of my stomach, so raw. Sometimes, I would be too scared to eat, knowing that it would trigger that level of pain that I had no control over and would have to wait until it started to subside. It wasn't like we ate junk food; my parents were really strict and food like cake or sweets were for, say, a weekend treat or a special occasion. I knew it wasn't due to that. It continued to get worse and then it started to affect my weight. Over the months, weight just started to drop off me. Seriously drop off me. I was eating and it was having no impact at all. I looked like someone who didn't eat. My clothes just hung off me. I tried changing my diet and cutting things out but it didn't make a difference. I couldn't work out what it was and no one else could either.

My parents would take me to the doctors, explain I was eating. However, they didn't believe them, and to be fair, if I saw someone who looked how I looked, I would have felt the same. The doctors started to monitor me and told me if my weight continued to fall, I would be admitted into hospital. That's the last thing I wanted; I didn't want to disrupt school. I was getting towards taking my GCSEs, and if I was going to become a barrister, I needed to get good GCSE grades as they would be taken into account for my A-levels and getting into university.

I felt that no one other than my parents believed me, which really upset me. There were so many whispers behind my back, the fake concern, the gossiping. The day of my nightmares came when the doctors told me my weight had got so low, I had to be admitted into hospital. The day they told me, I didn't want to go. I cried; I screamed; I had to literally be dragged out of the house as I held onto the door frames. I felt so bad for Mum and Dad; it would have been awful to see me like that, but what choice did they have but to let me go to the place where hopefully they could find some answers? I was worried my life was over and had been ruined.

The only thing I hoped was that by being in hospital, they could see I was in fact eating, which meant they could properly investigate what was wrong with me. My parents would bring me in food because the food was so bad. It wasn't the type of food that was going to build me up and make me feel better.

My parents were there all the time with me. I was so grateful to have them around. My mum was there from the minute she dropped my brother off at school to keep me company. She would leave in the afternoon to get my brother, then go home. Then my mum, dad and brother would return in the evenings and spend time with me. They were the only visitors I wanted. I hated visits from anyone else, the 'for show' visits from people that you would never normally see but who decided to make an appearance. They weren't visiting out of genuine concern; it was to be nosey and to gossip about me behind my back. I just wanted them all to go away; they didn't care normally so why care now?

I got my mum to ask the school to send me work so I wouldn't fall behind, plus it would give me something to do in the day. I was desperate to keep up with my education and have something that mentally stimulated me. Nothing much was going on in the hospital and whilst they gave you a PS1 to play on and a TV, there was only so much you could do before you were bored out of your brain.

That period I just felt trapped. Stuck on a children's ward where I was constantly monitored and judged by everyone except my mum, dad and brother.

Despite being supervised so the staff could satisfy themselves I was eating, I still continued to lose weight. My period stopped and everything. My weight got to under six stone, so low they suggested a drip. I refused and my parents refused. I wasn't doing that until they would investigate what was making me ill. My parents demanded they properly check what was wrong with me rather than writing this off as having an eating disorder. It was so hard to get our voices heard. No one believed me. The hospital even booked myself and my parents a taxi to go see an eating disorder unit over an hour away. We went, but I was never going there, and my parents weren't going to let me. I would have discharged myself from the hospital before I let that happen.

By the end of 1999, I had been in hospital for almost three months and was no further forward.

I spent NYE millennium night with my mum, dad and brother at the hospital. Everyone was freaking out about it turning midnight and about the millennium bug. What was going to happen? In fact, nothing happened, and after watching the fireworks, my parents and brother left me and went home.

I felt awful for my parents and brother, disrupting their lives and causing them worry. I felt so bad putting so much pressure on them. I just prayed, as I know they would have been, that in 2000, we would figure out exactly what was wrong with me and get me on the mend again.

2000

In the new year, we were determined we were going to push for some answers and solutions.

We persisted with the hospital to do a check – a body scan or anything – to establish the real reason for what was happening. Finally, someone listened and suggested an endoscopy. By this time, I had been in hospital for four months. I'm not sure if they agreed to do this because they believed us or more to shut us up. I think it was the latter. I wasn't only doing their head in but also my own.

I knew it would give me the answer that I needed and it did. I didn't have an eating disorder; I had coeliac disease. The reason why I was losing weight and so ill was because my body couldn't handle me eating wheat. That day, I cried because, finally, I knew what was wrong and I could now work on getting my health back. Whilst it was nice to prove people wrong, more importantly I couldn't wait to figure out how to feel better.

Coeliac disease wasn't something I had heard of. I didn't know where I was going to get the food from to eat. You couldn't just nip into the supermarket to get it. I learnt I could get food on prescription – like bread, flour and pasta – but that was about it. That food was horrendous. My mum was a good cook and cooked fresh anyway, so home-wise it wasn't an issue, but it seemed no one really knew how to cater for it, and that included within a hospital.

Now I had a plan of action, I could work on getting better. Though they couldn't let me go home until I reached at least seven stone, with the correct diet and not feeling constantly ill, I could achieve it. I remember, almost six months after being admitted, walking out of the hospital. It felt so weird to have my freedom again. I was still thin but not as bad as I had been. It took me until month six until I felt strong enough to go back to school. I really needed to get back, though what kept me going throughout was doing the work that school sent me. It gave me that focus to keep going.

I remember going back to school really embarrassed over what happened, and it wasn't even my fault. What would people think of me? Would they judge me? Had I fallen so far behind that I would have to redo the whole year? I just quietly settled back in. Kept my head down and hoped no one would make a fuss. I then remember classmates getting up in one of my lessons and saying, "Welcome back, Lorraine." Then, everyone was clapping and shouting, which was so unexpected but so kind. I was so emotional after that, not that I let anyone see it, but that meant so much to me.

Even though I was doing my schoolwork whilst in hospital, I had so much to catch up on. It was clear I was going to have to work even harder to get decent GCSEs as I had missed some elements of the practical exams. There wasn't anything anyone could do about that, which meant I would have to work even harder in the written exam. I just prayed it hadn't put me at such a disadvantage that I couldn't undo the damage. I made sure I spent the summer studying my socks off to make sure that wasn't the case.

Starting back in September, I knew it was GCSE year. It was a big year. Things were getting more serious, and it was a year where I had to knuckle down to make sure I got decent grades.

The people in my school were nice, but when it came to the day-to-day in class, it could often be hard to learn. You had the quiet ones i.e. me, at a few desks at the front, and the rest were just noisy and loud. Some days it was a free-for-all, especially if a supply teacher was there. On those days, god help you in getting anything done. For someone like me, who needed a calm and quiet learning environment, it was an absolute nightmare. Not that I would tell anyone to shut up, as the hassle from that wouldn't be worth it, so the best thing to do was keep my head down and battle through.

However, an opportunity came up to go for extra lessons at Northampton School for Boys, and I was asked if I wanted to go. Of course I did – I practically bit their hand off. Anything that would help me to get the best possible chance in exams I would take. A few of us would get taken in a minibus from our school. It was a completely different learning environment where you could actually focus, concentrate and learn. I felt the difference. It gave me the knowledge and skill I wouldn't have gained otherwise. It helped me to make up ground that I had lost from being in hospital and also from not being able to concentrate in class.

I don't know where the time went at school that year. I kept my head down. I studied and revised at every possible spare moment that I could.

When exams finally came, I had done all I could do. I felt I had done my best. Then, that was it – school was over. Whilst people were disappointed, I was excited, and I couldn't wait to leave. I was ready to get onto my next chapter of getting A-levels done. I had decided to stay and do A-levels in sixth form at the same school. Hardly anyone else was staying, which meant that the class sizes would be small, which for me was perfect.

I spent the summer trying to distract myself from thinking about my results. I was working part-time to earn some extra money to go out at night. I was just discovering going out with my friends on nights out. Something we really shouldn't have been able to do but managed to get away with. To escape the fear of what my results would be, I joined my friend and her family that week in Blackpool, leaving my parents to be the ones to go and collect my GCSE results. I had asked them to open up the envelope, whilst I waited on the phone, and read it out to me. I was praying it wouldn't be bad, so I didn't let them down.

It wasn't bad. I received As and Bs. I was over the moon. I had the grades I needed to do my A-levels and I had got the best grades in the whole school. I knew how much that would have meant to my parents, and I felt so proud that I could show them that, despite the setback with my health I didn't let it hold me back. The relief I felt was unreal, and I knew now that I could focus on getting into sixth form and working on getting my A-levels.

Sixth form was really cool. I loved it – for starters, the green uniform – which looked good on no one – was ditched. It was about getting the work done and having fun along the way.

We would all go out together, drinks and nights out. We would hang out together in-between classes. I just felt so much more me, and the class sizes were so small, it was an environment I could learn and thrive in.

As my sixth form couldn't do all the lessons I needed to get into university, they would pay for my taxi to take me to and from Northampton College. In terms of helping me to learn and get the grades I needed, I had to hand it to them – they were fully committed and invested in making that possible, which was something I was really grateful for.

2001-2003

It was becoming even more real that I would be going to university. Mum and Dad said not to worry about the money side of it. They would do what they could. I knew I only had two years to try and also help save. I would have to get a student loan of £3,000 a year as that would help with accommodation costs and the cost of my books. However, I would need more than that to live. I decided I would use that time to work when I could. I would work every weekend and then all throughout any school holiday I had. When I wasn't doing that and studying, I was partying with my friends. Life was good.

The time came to apply for universities; I went to visit loads of different ones, getting on the train with my parents to visit the open days. I couldn't believe we were here even doing this. My parents were so proud, and I was so excited. For us, people with no experience of ever doing this, it was a totally different world.

The minute I hit De Montfort University in Leicester I knew it was the one. I loved it – the campus was great, not too massive, and the law department sounded good, having spoken to lecturers and current law students. After deciding that it was going to be one of the six universities I would apply to, I was later invited for an interview to see if I was suitable to be accepted there.

I brought my parents, who waited for me outside. Of course, I was terrified. Thoughts back to when I shared what I wanted to do when I was younger and being ridiculed for it were coming back to haunt me. They asked me so many questions. Why do you want to come here? Why do you want to study law? Why criminal law? Why do you want to be a barrister? The list went on. I knew I wanted it more than anything else in the world, so it was a topic I could talk about all day long. It was one of those rare times when someone listened to me; they didn't judge or think I wasn't capable. They believed that I could do it. I was pleased to find out I would get a place there for September 2003, provided I got the A-levels to get in.

Whilst I did party hard, when it came to studying I would knuckle down. This was everything to me. I remember spending days with my revision timetable mapped out, studying my heart out. The room was hot, and I only came out when my parents called me for lunch or dinner. I didn't mind exams, so I had no issue passing my AS levels to go on to get my A-levels in year two.

I didn't want it to be over so quickly, but it was flying, which meant I was getting closer and closer to going to university. Something that terrified me as I would be leaving the safety net of home and being forced into the real world. I didn't have a choice but to go to university. I knew Leicester wouldn't be too far away from home either. At least I didn't have far to go back if it got too much.

I then started to really focus on what work experience was going to help me to get into the position I needed, to build the connections that I needed to get into a world where I had none. I wrote to absolutely everyone – judges and barristers' chambers – to ask if I could just sit and observe. I did get responses and opportunities, which I made sure I did during my school holidays.

I had work experience at the Old Bailey court shadowing a judge and week-long work experience at barristers' chambers in London. I was using my money earned from my Saturday job to travel and support from my parents. My parents were nervous about me taking the train down on my own, going back and forth each day. Trying to figure out the tubes was a nightmare. I'm surprised I made it anywhere with the number of times I got lost, ending up somewhere I shouldn't be. I was terrified, not that I let my parents know as I didn't want them to put a stop to it. I needed to do it. If this was what I wanted, I had to push myself forwards.

The work experience was another world. It was interesting and exciting when you were in the courtroom. It was just like I had imagined, although it confirmed to me that I didn't want to defend anyone at all. With some of the offences I was hearing, I just couldn't. Other barristers, solicitors and judges were encouraging, giving suggestions and tips to make it happen.

I was worried about not fitting in outside the courtroom. I wasn't interested or excited by the things that people were talking about, which was predominately law or politics. Conversations where I had no clue what they were on about or was not particularly interested in. A lot of the conversations I felt were more for show, rather than genuinely being interested in the other person. I hadn't anything to offer in these conversations, which meant I was super quiet, and they probably thought I was stupid. My world was just so different from theirs and I didn't feel like I belonged in that 'club'. It made me worry that when I was ready to do the job, I would be rejected on that basis.

However, those experiences identified the clear barrier that I would face, and that was money.

Being in that real-life legal environment made me want to do it more, so it wasn't the case I didn't want to do it. The reality was hitting home – how was I going to fit in or afford it? My parents were doing the best they could to support my dream, and I could never expect any more than they were giving. I was saving, but would that be enough for after university when I entered the world of work?

Just travelling down to London cost £30 a day. The salary for a trainee criminal barrister was £10,000 for the year. By the time I had paid the train, I would be left with £0. I would be continuing to build on the large debt that I already knew I would have when I left university and barrister training school. Living in London wasn't even an option. £10,000 wouldn't even cover the rent, never mind using the tube to get to courts. I was earning more than that now working in a bakery. Effectively, I would be working for nothing. A really upsetting thought, especially when everyone's perception is that you're going to be rolling in it. That was far from the case.

It made me think a lot about whether I should switch things up and do something else. I didn't tell my parents that as I didn't want them to feel bad. However, I thought this was the only time in my life, being young and with no real responsibilities, that if I was going to give it a go, wrack up debt and fail, then it was the best time to do it. At least if it all went wrong, I had somewhere to live and could find alternative employment to earn what I needed.

I decided to pursue it and see what happened; I was sure a plan would come together, and I would have to work really hard at making it happen. I wasn't scared of hard work. The A-levels came round quicker than I could ever have imagined. I needed to get the grades to get into De Montfort University, so the pressure was on. I couldn't have studied harder or done more than I had already when I did my final exam.

Then that was it, those two years over in the blink of an eye. It was a waiting game for results day. I was so glad it was over. I was going to miss Trinity, a place that had become a part of my life for so many years.

* * *

That summer consisted of working and partying to get through to the day when the results would be released.

Then, results day came, and I went in with my friends to collect them. I opened that envelope and realised I had done it. I got the grades to get in. I was so happy, so happy. Everyone said that was the happiest they'd ever seen me. Everyone knew how much it meant to me to get there. Then it really became real.

I would be leaving home in a month. Leaving my family behind and having to look after myself. I was scared as hell about doing that. We started buying things that I would need. I was going from Mum and Dad pretty much doing everything for me, to having to learn how to do this for myself. I could cook, so at least they were satisfied I wasn't going to live on crap or waste away.

I had no clue what to expect, no idea what the people I was going to live with were going to be like. Was I even going to like them? How unlucky would that be if I didn't? When I spoke to people who were going to university, one of the main aims was just to have the student experience; my focus was to do what it took to pass, or all of this would have been a waste of time.

Leaving home was so hard, travelling up with my parents. Loads of people all moving in. Everyone seemed nice, but I just wanted to go back with my parents, but I couldn't. I remember after they left feeling sad. I had always been around them. That night, we all went to the student union for a night out. It was weird going on a night out with people I didn't know and had only just met. I just hoped in time they would grow into friends.

I knew the next few years were going to be interesting, but I was in touching distance now of what I wanted to achieve, so now it was a case of making it a reality.

2004-2006

My three years at university flew by in a blur. For two years, I had never been out so much in my life. That was between Northampton, coming home to go out with friends, and Leicester. I was still able to hold down lectures, study, work and party – a pretty crazy cycle. Something you can only do when you're young.

However, I was enjoying it, and I was hitting the 2:1 mark; so as long as that wasn't impacted, I could cope. My student debt was escalating, not being helped by banks constantly offering overdrafts and credit cards. Without my parents there, who would have told me absolutely not to do this, I went wild. It was something I had never had before. The end result was that I accumulated far more debt than necessary.

It was before starting my final year, after finishing for the summer, that I met Lee. I was home for the summer. A three-month break. I spent the time working in the day and going out at night. My friend and I decided to go out on a Wednesday night, a really popular student night in Northampton, even though a large number of those people weren't students.

I was in NB's Bar, which was very popular on a Wednesday night, and we were on the dance floor. Two guys came over, dancing towards us, and started up a conversation. My friend loved to dance and one of them told her he was a professional dancer, so for her, I knew this was a challenge she would most certainly take on.

Lee being the other was also trying to keep up pace, and I thought they were both interested in my friend, but we had a good night dancing away. At the end of the night, Lee walked us both to the taxi, said goodbye and asked for my number. We messaged after that, went for a drink and some lunch, but I knew I was going back to uni. Third year, my plan was to knuckle down and focus on my work; I couldn't afford to mess it up. However, there was no chance of that happening as he went quiet on me and just disappeared. I was upset but just put my head into gear – it was time to get my degree. I didn't have time for distractions.

I did just that. I put my head down and studied. I had to rein in my party animal status, which was hard when you were constantly being asked to go out. There wasn't anything worse than knowing pretty much everyone in your whole building seemed to be going out except you, and you could hear them having the time of their lives outside. I did feel a loser and had to force myself to not change my mind. At the end of the day, I had to keep reminding myself why I was there, and it wasn't to get a degree in socialising. The library became my second home day and night.

Lee did get back in contact one day out of the blue, asking to meet a few months later. I told him he could come up to Leicester and he did on the bus. I met him at the bus station, I showed him around, and from then on, we were together.

Either he came up and stayed in Leicester or, as soon as my lectures were over, I would get the bus home to Northampton. He supported me throughout; he knew how important this was to me, and I couldn't have him as a part of my life if he was going to mess this up. He didn't – he supported me every step of the way. He blended so seamlessly into my life, I forgot what it was like not to have him there.

During my final year of university, I had to apply for my barrister training course so that I could start it the following September. I looked it up and knew it was going to cost me £9,000 to do the course alone. That was without books, travel, accommodation, etc. I chose to go to Bristol, the main factor being that it was the cheapest place to do the course. The rest were in London, starting at £12,000, and I had already identified how costly it would be to go to London.

I decided I was going to drive there back and forth. I had enough money to get a small car, a Kia Picanto. I realised I didn't want to live away from home anymore. I didn't want to spend another year in university accommodation or living a student lifestyle. I just wanted some normality, and I didn't want to escalate the debt more than it already was. I had my family and wanted to stay with Lee. If travelling back and forth, which I imagined would be no more than a couple of days a week for a year, was what it took, then that's what I would do.

It couldn't be rammed down your throat enough that if you didn't get a minimum 2:1 grade, then you shouldn't even bother doing a course and you would be unlikely to get a legal job. That put the fear in me. I studied so hard for exams so I could get in. I locked myself off. I survived on red bull and pro plus, which in hindsight wasn't a great combo as it left me a nervous wreck, with days of not being able to sleep. I was scared when exam time arrived; I was also relieved because it meant that soon it would finally be over. Once they were done, that was it, three years done in a blink of an eye. Now it was just a waiting game.

I was going to miss university. One of the most fun periods of my life. I had come out with so much debt: over £20,000 and I was only twenty. However, I didn't regret that at all. I had to do it to come out the other side. I remember packing up and leaving university, thinking I only had another chapter to close and that would be it.

That summer, the results came out and I had got a 2:1. I cried – I couldn't believe it. I was one more step away from achieving my dreams. Graduation day was amazing. My parents came, and my brother and Lee. The first time we had all been together. They'd all been a part of my journey, plus the 'meet the parents' could take place in a neutral setting. It was such a beautiful day, a chance to celebrate, and I was over the moon to get to a moment and a place which I had been told I wouldn't reach.

I knew the final step of becoming a barrister was hard and expensive. I got out a £25,000 professional studies loan from HSBC to fund it so I knew at the end of this I had better make it work, as I was knee-deep in debt. By the time I had finished, I would start real life £50,000 in debt, which I knew would take me a minimum of fifteen years to pay off. However, what choice did I have? If I didn't take it, then uni would have been for nothing. Passing the barrister training course and getting a career in law wasn't even an option without racking up this much debt.

I didn't realise how long the journey to Bristol would be

back and forth until I put it in my sat nav the day before I was due to go. I wish I did my research as I had completely underestimated how far it was and my heart sank at the thought of a six-hour round trip. I couldn't do anything about it now. All the accommodation had gone on campus. I couldn't backtrack now and tell my family and Lee I had made a mistake; I just had to get on with it. I just had to think, *I will do this six-hour round trip for a year and hopefully it isn't a course that I have to go and do every day.* Again, I was wrong. It was five days a week.

Day one, we all filled the lecture hall. On that course, there were 140 people in the room, all determined to succeed, but it became clear that not all of us would. They said that out of all of us in the room, only 25% of us at best would go on to have a legal career. I felt sick. No one had ever said this out loud or been so blunt before. I had been completely naïve that there was a job for all of us and we were all going to skip off into the sunset and do our dream career.

I looked around the room at people who were wealthier than me and had clear family connections that I didn't have and who appeared to have this ability to appear super intelligent, leaving me feeling inferior. They had a self-confidence that I had never had and didn't know how to go out and get. Just being there reminded me of how I felt when I did my work experience in London: out of place. I doubted whether I was good enough or cut out for this.

I completely underestimated how intense the course would be full-time compared to university. It was so hard, made harder by the fact I chose to drive back and forth to Bristol each day. I would leave home at 6am to get there for 9am for my lessons. Just praying the traffic wasn't too bad either way. Then I would leave at 3pm to get home by 6pm. I also had to study in the evenings. I wish uni had been a bit more intense to prepare me for this as I was absolutely knackered. I just kept thinking, *it's only a year; it will go fast.* Everyone was saying how wrecked I looked, and I was. Not that I would tell anyone how much I was really struggling; I just kept up the pretence it was all fine.

2007

I seemed to be doing well on my course even if I was finding it hard. I just kept my head down. However, me just getting on with it seemed to aggravate someone, who took it upon themselves to find ways to slowly knock down my confidence in the most subtle way. There were comments about my personality and my abilities. 'You're too quiet', 'are you going to be able to get a job after?', 'when you speak you shouldn't do or say that'. I had never had someone, let alone a grown adult who was far older than me, target me in a way that was clearly bullying like that. I couldn't work out what I had done, other than exist, to make someone be like that towards me. However, the impact was that it did make me start to doubt the confidence and belief I had in myself at the start of the course. I just completely shut down, attended class and left as soon as I could get out of there to get back home.

The thing that really made me angry was that it was done in such a way that you wouldn't have even known. I didn't know what to do. Did I report it? If I did, would they either not believe me or tell me to toughen up? I decided to tell no one.

It was made worse when I went to a lecturer asking for some advice on how I could increase my score on an assignment but was told I wasn't up there with the stars, but I should hopefully be able to pass. Then I started to think that maybe that person who was treating me this way was right, if even the person teaching me felt this way.

It made me feel not good enough to be there. I thought, *if this is what people in this world are like, do I actually even want to be part of it? Am I always going to be treated like this?* But how could I have gone back then and said I didn't want to do it anymore?

Running alongside this course, you had to do 'dining sessions' which all took place in London. These were twelve mandatory dinners that you would have with senior lawyers and fellow students like yourself. There would be talks, dinners and networking opportunities. There were four places that held this in London, and I selected the Inner Temple. Not only was it a beautiful place, but it did seem welcoming for people with my background. You couldn't pass the course without doing this.

You would bring a guest with you for lunch or dinner, or sometimes you would go on your own. It was very formal. You would hope that on those occasions you had to attend, you could seek out people like you, who hadn't experienced anything like this before. Like me, they stood out a mile; you would gravitate to each other and at least you could have a laugh and feel normal.

Combining the dining sessions with how I felt about my course, that year being over couldn't come soon enough. I had never travelled so much in my whole life, with my little Kia Picanto taking me everywhere.

The final thing I had to do before I qualified was find someone who was a barrister to sign a form to say I was suitable to become a barrister. A supporter. Someone who could sign off my form to say I was suitable to be put forward to be a barrister. I knew no one and I had to find someone pretty quick. So, I just started looking up barristers' chambers and started to write to people, hoping that someone would get back to me because if they didn't, it didn't matter whether I passed the course or completed the dining sessions, I wouldn't be able to become a barrister anyway.

One lady, Fiona, did write back to me. She invited me to come down to London and speak with her. I remember getting on the train down and praying she would agree to sign it for me because I really didn't know what I was going to do if she didn't. She was so lovely and kind. She asked questions about me, what I wanted to do and where I wanted to go. She agreed to sign it for me and said she would come along to support me on the night. At least, out of the whole year, that was one positive: someone thought I was capable.

I don't know where the year went doing that course, but it went in a blur. Though it was a year that I was glad was over.

I didn't leave the course thinking I had done my best. I hadn't as, that summer, for the first time in my whole life, I had failed an exam which meant I couldn't pass. The letter came to my house; I was shocked. It said I had two chances to get this one exam right or that would be it. I was really angry with myself as I had let people's negative attitude towards me knock my confidence to the extent that I didn't do my best or put my all into something I really wanted.

Now I wasn't in that negative environment, around people I didn't want to be around, I was going to try and turn it around. I had to turn it around as this was the final hurdle. I didn't have another £9,000 to do the whole thing all over again.

So, I was determined I would use the summer to work my socks off in passing that resit. I had wanted this more than anything. I worked so hard that when I took my exam, I was more than ready for it. I knew I had passed it and when the letter came through that I had, it was time to prepare for graduation from the course, but also, I could finally get called to the Bar. I could finally officially become a barrister. I cried. I was over the moon; I had done it. All those people, for all those years who told me I couldn't get to this moment. I just couldn't believe it, and my parents were so happy, telling me they always knew I would do it.

I had two ceremonies to attend to make it official.

The first ceremony at Bristol was to graduate from my barrister course. It was in Bristol cathedral, an absolutely spectacular building. I drove my mum and dad there. All those journeys on my own to those classes back and forth, without my parents realising how long that drive was for me. They were shocked. I was thinking, *how the hell did I manage to do this for a year, even in those winter months when the weather was bad?* I would never be doing that journey again if I could help it.

Even in those moments, the moments I was so proud, there were comments from other families – 'she looks more like she should be doing modelling than becoming a barrister'. I tried ignore it, but it bothered me why people were so concerned with what other people were doing instead of focusing on themselves.

It didn't stop it from being a real proud moment, not only for me but also for my parents – the two people who had been my cheerleaders throughout.

The next ceremony at the Inner Temple in London was incredible and everything I imagined it to be when I wanted to set out to do this. I drove down with Lee and my parents to the ceremony. There was free-flowing drink; I got to catch up with people from my course. It was the most amazing feeling. Fiona, who had signed my form, kept to her word and came down to see me and support. She was wonderful and told me to stay in touch should I ever need anything. The champagne and wine were flowing, my parents taking full advantage. This meant the drive home consisted of my dad singing and my mum saying she felt sick. It was so funny. They deserved it after all they had been through to support me and make this moment possible.

So, I was twenty-one now and I was qualified. It was time to get out into the real world. It was weird not studying for something or not having anything to focus on working towards. I applied for pupillages (barrister training positions) but was unsuccessful. I was upset by that because I wanted to get stuck in and I thought that the work experience I had gained would have been enough – it wasn't. I wasn't sure what more I needed to do to successfully pass an interview, and now that I was completely out of the university environment, I had no one really to turn to now either. I was on my own, and I realised if this was something I wanted to do, I was going to have to get out in the world and try to seek it out myself.

I had finished all my studies with a student debt hitting the £50,000 mark. I had a one-year break before my professional studies loan repayments kicked in and my student loan would start coming out of my wages at a percentage they deemed appropriate as soon as I started working. I worked out it would most likely take me fifteen years to pay it back, a scary thought.

I was lucky that I could return home to my parents to remove that financial worry and pressure to sort myself out. I couldn't just sit there waiting, so I got a job at Victim Support as a volunteer manager in the meantime. I'm not sure how I did as I had no experience.

It was a great entry point into getting an understanding of the criminal justice process. An opportunity to see it from the other side. So, it wasn't wasted experience as it gave me the background and insight which would help me when I did eventually get the job that I wanted.

The job was always a stopgap job for me but one where I really enjoyed being able to earn a salary and get some life stability. However, a job advert came up for a Magistrates Court Legal Adviser. I would actually get to use the qualification I trained for. I would be advising the magistrates in court who weren't legally qualified on matters of criminal law. It was perfect, and it was local – even better. I decided to go for it.

This would be my first proper job. In the interview, I was grilled to death by a panel of three to the point I thought they must hate me, but I didn't back down. I guessed that was what it would be like in court. Despite feeling I had failed on leaving, I couldn't believe it when I was told I had been successful. I knew I would use this time to get the knowledge and skills so that I could do the job I really wanted, which was to be a prosecutor for the CPS, and I wanted to work in London.

So, it had taken my initial dream, aged ten, until twenty-two to start to make the things I wanted finally happen. It would have been so easy to give up and listen to all those people who told me it wasn't possible. I'm glad I didn't – I made it. I couldn't wait to see what the next chapter of my life would bring.

PART 2

2010

2010. New year, new decade. The year had started off great. We got married at our dream wedding venue Fawsley Hall. It was the perfect day, the day we always wanted. The weather even held out for us. We were surrounded by our family and friends. Followed by a wonderful trip to Jamaica for our honeymoon.

We knew this would be the start of the next chapter of our lives, full of hope and promise.

The legal adviser job was going OK, despite the initial baptism of fire. Starting that job, I realised how much legal training didn't prepare you for the world of work and how little I knew. It was sink or swim and I was just in the early stages of swimming. Still finding my feet.

I had bought a house too. Financially it was tight as I was still paying off the student debt at over £500 a month and my mortgage was £800. Money was seriously tight; I couldn't get the debt down because we kept doing and buying stuff that we didn't really need. An appearance thing that we were doing really well, even though financially, due to my student debt payments, it was so hard.

Life just took its normal routine of home and work. Nothing was exciting or really stood out, it was just ordinary.

However, never did we expect our life to change so shortly after our wedding. Yet it did, like a lightning bolt completely taking us by surprise, and it would change our life forever. That change was *cancer*.

It was June, a few months after we had got married. I was at work in court when Janice, my mother-in-law, phoned to tell me she had been diagnosed with cancer. In all honesty, I can't remember the conversation. Once the word cancer had been mentioned, my brain had already shut down and I was thinking the worst. All these questions in my head. What do I even say? How can I provide some reassurance? How was life going to change? How would Lee be? I remember being told to tell Lee. I really didn't want to, but having just been told that, how do you say, "No, can't you do it?"

I did phone Lee, who was also at work. I know I told him, but again I couldn't tell you what I said, but his response was OK, and he seemed fine, like I had asked him, "Can you grab me something from the shop on your way home from work?"

I left it at that, completing the afternoon at work in a daze. I was wondering what was going to happen now. I eventually was able to go home. Luckily, it was a day when we could in fact finish early.

However, when I got home, things weren't OK. Lee wasn't in a good way. He was a mess; he couldn't stop crying and saying over and over that his mum was going to die. He had drunk two bottles of wine. One, Lee doesn't drink wine and two, Lee would have never touched my wine as I would have kicked off. Nothing I could do or say made it any better. I felt useless and hopeless, trying to reassure him everything was going to be fine when deep down I felt that was a lie. I had never been in this situation before. If I was going by the limited experience that I did have, which was based on fictional TV and films, then she was going to die, and he was right.

I called his parents to come and help because I couldn't offer the comfort he clearly needed, and they did. They were able to calm him down, reassure him and get him under control. They seemed to take it in their stride – well, surface level they appeared to be handling it. Which I guess was reassurance enough for me.

I can't remember the words exchanged between us that day at all. It was like a silent film. I can picture it and see everything that happened, and it was obvious what was happening, but I couldn't tell you a word that was said.

I couldn't stop thinking about how, at our wedding, she had been telling us about these lumps. The ones that had started to become visible, but she thought they were cysts. Even on that day, it had been there then. How could we not have realised this sooner? Should we have pushed this? Had I been too wrapped up in the wedding and buying a house to notice what was right before my eyes? It would have been too easy to start playing the blame game but right then, where was that going to get us? What were we actually going to achieve from it?

Following being told Janice had cancer, treatment started pretty much straight away. She had been diagnosed with Non-Hodgkin's Lymphoma and it was really aggressive.

The thing was, for ages, she had these lumps appearing around her body, which we now realise were in her lymph nodes. The belief was that they were cysts, even though they appeared to continue growing. I remember on my wedding day that she had a lump that had appeared on her neck and was saying how painful it was. So, it had been there for a while.

Once the truth was finally discovered, the hospital moved onto trying to get it sorted straight away. We couldn't fault them on that. To be honest, we never really got involved in going to the sessions for chemotherapy. Janice and Chris, my father-in-law, would go together. We would ask how it was going and they would tell us it was fine. They were really positive, and if they had been thinking something different, you wouldn't have been able to tell. Even if we had wanted to go, our jobs wouldn't allow it. We both had jobs that were long hours: a chef and a lawyer. There were no guaranteed finish times, breaks or flexibility.

However, Janice did start to look ill, the gradual changes that you expect with someone going through treatment. Changes to skin, what foods you eat and starting to experience loss of hair. I had only seen this on TV and not in person, so no one in 'real life'. So, it was a real shock to me, but I of course masked that. I didn't want her to feel worse than she already did.

I remember when the hair loss became so bad that Janice decided it was time to shave off all of her hair. We made a big deal of it, a family event with everyone being invited to come round. I don't know what she really felt because you couldn't tell, but I know for a fact I would have been petrified. Before her hair was shaved off, it was easier to put it out of your mind what was happening and pretend that she didn't have cancer, but once her hair had gone, it made it feel real. Different people took turns to shave off her hair until none was left.

Lee called her a slap head. There was that moment when it was completely silent, where I was thinking Lee was going to get slapped, and to be honest, I thought he was on his own with this one as everyone looked at each other, waiting for her reaction. Even he wasn't sure if he had gone too far that time as he looked unsure. Then she started laughing and we all did. It's crazy how you can create a funny memory out of what was a sad moment.

Yet she still remained positive, something I really admired.

Life continued with the hope that the chemotherapy would do the job and we could all get back to our normal lives and put this situation behind us.

However, it didn't. The effect of treatment meant she now started to have hospital stays on our local cancer ward in Northampton. Not visiting wasn't an option, even though I was nervous and scared. I would be lying if I said I wasn't. However, I felt that way because I didn't know what to expect. What did I say? How did I speak? Where did I even look?

I raised it with my parents who said, "Why would any of that be an issue? Just go in and be yourself. Act how you would want to be treated." I then knew I had to fix up, sort myself out and get on with it.

It didn't stop me feeling nervous, though, as we entered the ward. There were people at various stages of diagnosis. Some people looked seriously ill, whilst others you couldn't tell they had cancer. I had expected a horrible atmosphere and a sense of death but that totally wasn't the case at all. Everyone was really nice and friendly. The nurses were lovely and kind, looking out for everyone. It was actually OK. People were smiling and people said hello and it was fine.

It was just normal, everyday people. I actually felt ashamed that I had been so scared.

We spent quite a lot of time visiting the ward. Over that time, we noticed so many wonderful acts of kindness, for instance the lady who would come in and give free head, hand and foot massages to patients. Not only that, but she would have a lovely chat with them too. She just did this out of the kindness of her heart to make people feel better.

There was a man that would come round with food and drink treats. How amazing was that? He again wanted nothing in return, he just did it because he was kind.

I had never really witnessed or experienced people giving their time to help others, not because they had to but because they wanted to. You never hear publicly about these people; they quietly get on with making a difference to others. These gestures made the ward even more special, and I was grateful that my mother-in-law was there. It was a place filled with so much love and acts of kindness.

They definitely demonstrated that to her. We were conscious that visiting was four hours and, due to all our work commitments, we could only do the evenings. So, knowing that there were people on the ward looking out for someone you loved at least gave you some sense of comfort from the guilt of not being able to do more.

2011

Yet treatment continued and she never seemed to be getting any better; if anything, she seemed to be getting worse. From diagnosis to summer 2010, it felt like Groundhog Day in that respect. I couldn't see any real progress or improvement that was enough to say this treatment was working. We couldn't challenge what was going on either as we didn't know exactly what was being said at the appointments. Then Lee and I were starting to question what was really going on because when we asked, we weren't getting any answers.

But that summer we did get answers: treatment wasn't working, and the only option now to save her life was a bone marrow transplant. It wasn't really an option when you looked at it. You have a bone marrow transplant, and you live, or you don't and die. Also, only one of you out of the group of six people who were having the bone marrow at the time was likely to survive, and the odds were very limited. I'm not sure what more the doctor could have said to have woken us up to the realities of the situation. However, I don't fault the doctor for his honesty. The honesty was needed, and the realisation hit home hard how bad things were. They were a lot worse than we thought.

So, the option was the bone marrow transplant, even though there was the risk she wouldn't make it. However, what other option did you really have? We all prayed it would work to put an end to all of this. That was the only thing at that particular moment that could work. That one in six thought stayed at the back of our minds.

We didn't even need to test if one of the family was a suitable match for the bone marrow. Someone was found relatively quickly. Someone from Australia, a male who was the perfect match. We were extremely lucky as not everyone is so fortunate to find a match straight away. This had to happen to avoid risking losing the donor. It had been made clear to us that there was really no time to waste.

The thing with having the bone marrow transplant is that it wouldn't be at our local hospital. She would be moved to Leicester Royal Infirmary, which was around an hour away on a good day, minus traffic. Whilst an hour each way might not seem far, it is when you're working all day, then having to go home. Plus, it wasn't a case of just rocking up – due to the ward being one where people were at high risk of infections, you had to make sure you went home, got changed and showered before even making your way there. You had to do all that and still try to make it so you had enough time to see the person before visiting ended at 8pm.

Then you had the added cost of petrol, parking, food, essentials and activities you were bringing up to keep the person occupied in hospital. All this, and you had to factor in the fact that the person in hospital could no longer work, so you had a loss of income. It was so hard.

It was stressful. The job I was in at the time became more and more frustrating for me with not knowing what time I would finish. My finish time was dictated by when the court finished and not by my personal needs. They were irrelevant. Yes, I know that's what I signed up for, but that was before I had any real responsibilities. It also meant I couldn't really go to the hospital because I could say I would be there, but the reality was I knew it would be a day where I finished late. I couldn't expect anyone to wait for me, at the risk of letting everyone else down if I had to turn around on the day and say I couldn't make it.

Lee during this time decided to change his job as, with the hours, it just wasn't working, and family came first. So, he worked at a café where he finished at 4pm, so he could go with his dad to the hospital as soon as he finished work.

So, I would get the updates about what was happening and how it was going. Once the bone marrow happened in November 2011, things got really bad because her body started to reject the bone marrow. Something we had been told could happen. The people in the group of six who had their bone marrow transplants were dying one by one. We were wondering if she would be one of them.

There were so many times when the hospital would call to say you needed to get to the hospital as they didn't think she was going to make it. You were always preparing yourself for the worst news. Yet somehow, Janice would always pull through, which was amazing, but we were constantly nervous wrecks as we just didn't know what was going to happen.

I couldn't even begin to imagine what it must have been like for her, lying in a room spending all that time on your own when you felt so unwell and without your loved ones around you. What stopped me from feeling useless for not being there enough to care for her was knowing that there was a team of hospital staff who did an amazing job at being our extended family. The people looked after her 24/7. They were so compassionate, kind and caring and treated people as if they were a member of their own family. These people were true angels who gave so much, way beyond what their job description told them they should do.

It became clear that she would be spending Christmas in hospital, something that anyone we had ever met dreaded. Something we had hoped would never happen. No one wants to spend Christmas in hospital, speaking to anyone who had been in hospital around that period, it was a really great fear.

We knew Christmas day was going to be awful, to top off what had already been a horrible year. Janice would still be in Leicester, so we would drive up to see her on Christmas Day. How could you not? Knowing Christmas wasn't going to really be like Christmas, Lee and I decided to have a mini-Christmas together on Christmas Eve, staying in the place we got married, Fawsley Hall. It was so festive and so beautiful. However, it was really painful as there were families everywhere together enjoying each other's company and celebrating this time of year. Just as we normally would. If anything, it made me feel sad about our situation. If Lee thought the same, I never knew because he didn't say it, but I had a sense that he did.

The next day, we left, spent some time with my parents and had dinner with them. Then we made our way up to Leicester to do our Christmas Day hospital visit.

It was just the four of us there: me, Lee, Janice and Chris. The only indication that it was Christmas was the way Chris, Lee and I were dressed up, trying to bring some joy into a situation where there really was none, but you had to do what you could to stay positive. We did present swaps, but Janice couldn't even get up to open her own presents, so Chris had to do it for her. She couldn't move or speak. There was no real interaction between us. She just lay there as she was so ill, so upset at being ill and just crying without sound. It was painful as you felt so useless – there was absolutely nothing you could do, and she was in the hands of whatever was being given to her to help her recover. Hopefully, her body was strong enough to get better.

The whole visit just left me feeling flat. After spending a few hours there, we drove back. It felt awful that we all drove home, leaving her behind, spending Christmas Day night alone. I couldn't stop thinking what must have been going through her head right then.

We all thought that next year it would be better. We would make it extra special to make up for it.

2012

At the start of January 2012, Janice started to improve. The bone marrow seemed to be working, which was good. It was baby steps but good baby steps – it felt like things were heading in the right direction. Then, eventually, two months later, she was finally allowed to come home. Any further hospital admissions or check-ups to be done in Northampton. This was great news for us all as she would be closer to home. Coming home didn't mean life going back to normal, though, because her body had no immune system.

Life for her was going to be so different: isolation to prevent risk of an infection meant she couldn't leave her house; windows had to be shut and contact with others kept to a minimum. She had to wear a mask if she had to go outdoors, being careful with her diet, and the list goes on. It was so restrictive, and it would be that way for a period of one year. However, it didn't matter as at least she would be home and that was the main thing.

Whilst there were hospital trips and stays, it felt like we were turning a corner and things were starting to feel like they were going to get a bit better.

Then, in April 2012, something happened that knocked the wind completely out of us. Doreen – who was Janice's mum, Lee's grandma – passed away when she had an operation. It was so sudden. Something none of us expected would happen. It was a shock for sure when we were told. It was a knock-back for us all, especially Janice in terms of her health. It declined; with the combination of recovering from a bone marrow transplant and grief, it was too much. So much sadness at the time we thought life was going to start getting better.

The funeral was a reminder of an amazing person we had lost as we sat there listening to the service and learnt so much about her. I remember seeing Chris crying, which was rare as he never showed any real emotion publicly or in the last two years since Janice was diagnosed with cancer. Seeing him this way shocked us. He said it was because, after everything that had happened, it could have been Janice there right then, which broke my heart as it made me realise he wasn't as tough as he made out to be. That was a really rare glimpse into how he was feeling. We had completely underestimated how hard this must have been for him, putting on this brave face, not confiding in anyone how he felt and trying to keep it together all the time.

After the funeral, it felt like we pretty much took up some temporary residence in Northampton hospital. We were in and out like a yoyo with Janice, something we had been warned of.

Over the next few months, Chris started to feel unwell, constantly ill and always having chest pains. Lee started to step in to cook and leave him meals because we didn't believe he was getting time to eat properly or look after himself. He was going back and forth to the hospital, whilst still managing to hold down a job to pay the bills and help everyone else at pretty much every moment that he could. However, he was told it was a chest infection. He just cracked on. However, these pains never seemed to go away.

On 25 October we got a call – the chest pains were really bad, and he needed an ambulance. He was taken to hospital. We knew this was serious as there was no way he would want to be admitted into hospital, let alone stay in the hospital. I didn't go that night, but Lee did. I said I planned to visit the next day after work as it was a Friday. Lee came back and said he had had a heart attack. Words I never expected to hear. I was shocked; we all were because he had been suffering that long and, whilst we knew he was unwell, he didn't tell us he felt that bad. Lee said he seemed fine and was in good spirits; well, as good as you can be for someone who's just found out they had a heart attack. However, he said he was doing OK. It was weird to think of him in the hospital and Janice being out, when it was usually the other way round. The both of us planned to visit him after work the next day.

I remember going to bed that night with no further updates from the hospital. No news was good news, right? We thought everything was fine as far as we were concerned. However, I remember being woken up by the phone ringing. It was still dark, and I checked the time – it was 4.26am. Anyone ringing at that time could only be a bad thing and I felt sick; even before the phone was answered I just knew it was going to be bad. The phone continued to ring; Lee didn't want to answer it. I was trying to shake him awake. I knew he wasn't sleeping, and he was just telling me to ignore it. I know why, though, as we both thought the worst. I made him answer it and it was his mum telling him to go to the hospital as he needed to come and say goodbye.

On hearing those words, nothing after that felt real. The rest felt like some type of horrible dream as we got dressed and then I drove to pick up my sister-in-law Laura. We made small talk about God knows what, and I have no memory of the journey there. It was still dark when we walked into the hospital and the nurse huddled us all into the smallest side room I had ever seen. The four of us crammed in there. The situation reminded me of those shows you see on TV. The ones where you know if you're in this room it's only going to be bad news, and it was. He had had another heart attack, and he was only being kept alive by the breathing machines. It was our time now if we wished to go in and say goodbye before they turned them off.

Walking in, seeing him lying there covered in wires, what do you really say or do? It was just complete, utter shock. How can you go from one day being there to that being it? I had no words, and I couldn't believe this would be goodbye and that would be it. Leaving that room, knowing you will never see that person again alive. Leaving that room felt like life was over. Janice wanted to stay and so Lee, Laura and I left.

I remember driving home; by that time it was light and a normal Friday morning – everyone was driving to work, and we were driving home. We were all supposed to be at work.

Life on the outside looked normal, but it really wasn't. I seemed to be the one who had been appointed as being the person in charge, even though I had no real clue what I was supposed to do or say. I felt sick doing this. I was ringing round to let everyone know and they were all in genuine shock, complete disbelief – was I sure, did I mean Janice?

As everyone was coming to Janice and Chris's house, we only had a small window to return home ourselves to try and get our head round what the hell had just happened. In those moments, the tears came. I wasn't able to offer any words of comfort to Lee other than to cry with him, which probably was of no help whatsoever, but I didn't know what else to do. We sorted ourselves out, went back to their home and welcomed everyone in who came to pay their respects.

It felt like he had just nipped out and would be back soon and not be gone forever. None of us could believe what had happened. The whole thing felt like one of those nightmares which you wished you could wake up from, rather than this being real.

That night we stayed at the house, in their room. We couldn't leave Janice by herself. I was terrified and I stayed awake all night. All his things were set out as if he was about to come back. I kept thinking he going to jump out and say it was one big joke. However, that moment never came.

The days blurred into weeks as we tried to process what had happened. There was a funeral to arrange. Lee and I took this on. We had no clue what we were doing and there was paperwork to sort. We couldn't expect Janice to do it; not only was she grieving, but she was unwell. All through this, we were thinking, *how is this even happening? We shouldn't have to be doing this.*

We went to see Chris at the hospital chapel. Before all this, seeing anybody dead would have totally freaked me out and I would have had nightmares for weeks; even my parents asked if I was sure I wanted to go. However, I had to go to support Lee, and a few of us went. When it was our turn to go in, it was just myself and Lee.

Chris was there in the middle of the room. I don't know what happened – I think the setting where we were, seeing him lying there, it was just all so final. Too much for me to handle after the weeks of just keeping myself busy.

Being in that room, I just felt I couldn't breathe, and it felt like my throat was closing off and no air would come in. I had to be taken out and I was really angry with myself and embarrassed as I was supposed to be there to support everyone and not the other way round.

Before we knew it, it was the day of the funeral. We went to say our final goodbyes beforehand, in the smallest room. Myself, Lee and Laura all crammed in. Chris was wearing the outfit that he was wearing Christmas Day the year before when we had all visited Leicester Royal Infirmary. Seeing him lying there, it was hard to imagine how we had got here and what had actually happened to our lives.

We made our way home, and all the family were there, waiting until the hearse arrived before making our way to the crematorium. We weren't sure how many people would turn up, but there were so many people who came to show their love and support. We had to stand there greeting people and thanking them for coming, whilst trying not to fall apart.

With so many people there, the room was completely full. We were totally blown away by it and he would have been too. It was a beautiful service, but it was hard. He was only fifty-one, so young. It just didn't feel right. It felt so wrong. We knew after this moment, life was going to be so different.

Then, after that, life went on, but it wasn't easy. Overnight, Lee and I knew we would have to look after Janice. It quickly became clear that we would do what we could to support with hospital visits and helping out, because that's what you do, even if it meant life had to change. We didn't realise how much he did and completely underestimated the pressure he was under. However, between the two of us, we would make it work, even if it meant lifestyle-wise, things would change, and they did.

Chris died and was cremated so close to Christmas. It wasn't a time of celebration; it was too raw. Christmas came and it was horrendous, even if we just tried to make the best of a bad situation. We couldn't wait for the year to end. It had been so painful. We weren't too sure how we could move forward from everything that had happened.

2013

I think the grief knocked Janice's positive mindset, which impacted on her health, and this made her really, really ill. She even ended up on the intensive care unit. We were praying that, as our start to the new year, she wasn't going to die too. By this stage, she was the only person alive from the group that had the bone marrow transplant. She was giving up and her mindset had gone from being determined to get better to not wanting to continue. When dealing with grief of two people you love, it was understandable. Any of us would have felt that way.

With Janice continually being ill, it meant we were always in the hospital. They might as well have issued a room so we could move in and live there because we were there so much.

I can't remember much from this period apart from feeling like I was on rotation work – hospital, home and sleep. It was hard going. It made us realise how tough it was for Chris to keep up with the daily routine on his own. Also, the expense that flowed from it – parking, items the person in hospital needed, travel costs, buying food to eat as you didn't have time to cook something – all these things hadn't even entered my mind.

Since Chris's death, our lives changed drastically. All the things we regularly did such as going on a night out and going away had to stop. There was no real time to socialise or do anything but work during the day to earn money and then be around after work to support. I had no issue with that; that's what needed to be done.

What surprised me, though, was that people didn't seem to get it. I would have rather people asked me 'do you fancy a coffee?' or 'do you need anything?' instead of, 'are you free tonight to go out?', especially when they knew my situation. It made me angry. I lost a lot of friends during that time. People who didn't get it. That it wasn't just the case my father-in-law had died but, because of his death, we had now become carers. A concept that some people just didn't seem to grasp.

When Lee and I didn't think any more bad news could come into our life, it did.

One night in February, we had gone to bed as normal. I remember Lee waking up in the middle of the night stating he could hear water running. I hated being disturbed sleeping, so I was pretty annoyed to be honest and told him to shut up and go back to sleep. He was imagining things.

However, next thing I remember, he was really shaking me to wake up and said there was water spraying everywhere.

I sat up, and this time, I could hear it too. I jumped out of bed and went to the bathroom to have a look. There was water shooting out the back of the toilet like one of those garden water sprinklers on full speed.

It had clearly been going on for hours. There was water everywhere. Walking downstairs, you stepped off the bottom step into water. We looked up – there were holes in the ceiling where water was pouring through into every room.

Everything we owned was soaked, every electrical item, piece of furniture, the flooring.

We just couldn't believe it. Why was this happening to us? We had only bought the house four years ago, and it was supposed to be brand new.

Lee managed to shut the water off. Both of us then worked in the dark, because the electricity was out, to try and clear up the water and deal with the damage. We couldn't really assess the damage as it was night-time. After a few hours, feeling we had done the best that we could, we tried to get a couple of hours of sleep before we went to work, thinking it would be fine.

Waking up the next day and seeing the house in daylight, it was wrecked beyond belief. The house was destroyed – the flooring had buckled up; the holes in the ceiling were bigger than I imagined; you knew you couldn't turn on any electrical item due to the risk of getting an electric shock; and all the furniture was damaged.

We were devastated. Everything we had ever worked for, all that debt we had got in was for what? There was pretty much nothing left that was OK apart from our clothes.

I remember contacting work and telling them what had happened. No response – I was fuming because that meant I had to go in. Lee couldn't get out of work either, so we both had to wave goodbye to the mess that was our home and try to focus on our day job. That was hard as we had so much to sort. Right then, we didn't have anywhere to live.

After an hour of getting to work to be told, 'I didn't think you were coming in' – which sent my stress levels through the roof – I returned back home and realised there was nothing I could do to salvage it.

The fault clearly lay with the builder not replacing a temporary waste pipe with a permanent one. It was literally a ticking time bomb as to when it was going to go off.

I was told my new build ten-year guarantee meant nothing in this situation, which was an actual shock to the system as, if it wasn't for situations like that, then what did it actually cover? Having now properly inspected it, not a great deal.

Thank God for the insurance company who immediately came out and said we couldn't live there and that it was going to take at least two months to dry out. Huge industrial drying heaters were put in that would be on 24/7 to try and dry it out before they could even think of rebuilding and redecorating. We watched everything we worked for being taken out and thrown into a skip.

Lee and I packed up our clothes into suitcases, and we were moved into the Premier Inn down the road, which was to become our home for the next four months. One family size room for us to live in, our belongings reduced to suitcases. We couldn't believe after everything that had happened to us, it had come to this. At the same time, we were all still grieving. Janice was still constantly in and out of hospital. We were trying to juggle day-to-day life after everything we had dealt with for the last two years. It just became too much to handle.

Janice didn't know the extent of what had happened. We didn't want to create any more worry and stress. We knew she couldn't handle it. We said we had a leak but didn't tell her the extent of it; we told her it was fine.

My parents helped, especially with washing and drying of clothes and food. Other than that, we were totally alone.

While people thought it was cool to live in a hotel, it really wasn't.

I couldn't explain how low I felt. We had been through so much since we got married. We hadn't even had a chance to enjoy our marriage. It had already been so tough, then this and then having to battle to get acknowledgement that this wasn't our fault.

That period made me ill. I started to get chest pains, which was to do with anxiety and stress. I felt genuinely unwell; with being coeliac, eating out in a way that was healthy was an absolute nightmare.

I knew the light at the end of the tunnel would come eventually, but the way I felt, it was just impossible to see it. I always worried what was going to happen next. What was going to go wrong?

It took four months for them to sort out our house; it was finally rebuilt to the way it should have been, after having unleashed a whole number of other problems in the rebuilding process. We just hoped this was finally a new beginning for us all.

2014

It was now coming up to four years since Janice's original diagnosis of cancer. The scary phase with the bone marrow was over. There were still the hospital admissions as a result, but everything looked more promising than it had done for the previous few years.

During those hospital stays, Janice would ask if we could bring her a TV from home so she could watch. We couldn't afford to pay for a TV for her, especially with the amount of time she was in hospital. We hoped that Janice would be amenable to a fourteen-inch TV from home, but we were wrong – the request was for the large thirty-two-inch one. Nothing makes you look dodgier than lugging a thirty-two-inch TV around like you robbed something, especially in a town centre and walking through a hospital. Of course, I made Lee carry it, but I still looked like an accomplice.

I really didn't want to get in a situation where we were stopped and asked questions. At the end of the day, would anyone really believe us? I wouldn't, and those are the type of scenarios I deal with in my day job. Yet, how could you say no when the response was 'Chris used to do it'? To be fair, he did, without question or fuss – he just did what needed to be done.

That was the moment I decided I knew what I could do to help others, especially after everything that had happened – I wanted to do something positive.

I knew a solution that would help people in hospital, which was to have free TVs for the wards. There were fourteen individual rooms on the ward, where people would be in isolation. It would just be them in the room. It could be because they were particularly vulnerable or unwell and this meant they had to be alone. There was a TV in the room, but as I already mentioned, you had to pay to watch it.

I'm sure we weren't the only ones who worried about affordability. However, the TV did help. It was something in the background or to watch to stop you feeling so disconnected and isolated. If it was going to help someone feel better in hospital, then I would find a way to raise the money I needed to fund them. I had never taken on a fundraising challenge myself before and wasn't sure how to fundraise, having never done it before.

Then, I thought about what I could do. I needed to do something that was a challenge and wasn't easy that would persuade people to sponsor me. I thought back to the previous summer when my brother had done Tough Mudder. He described how crazy it had been. How he had to go to the hospital for stitches to a cut to his hand afterwards. How people dropped like flies from the electric shock stations. Any normal person wouldn't have been sold by that, but I decided that was the thing I wanted to do and was going to do because it wouldn't only shock people, but it would also push me totally outside my comfort zone.

I needed to find someone who was willing to do it with me. Luckily, that came in the form of my friend Natalie, who actually really wanted to do it. If she hadn't paid my £100 entry for me, I do think I would have found a way to get out of it or tried to find something a bit gentler. However, the commitment was now there, and I had to pay her the £100 back.

I remember telling people I was going to do it and asking if they could sponsor me. People laughed; people questioned whether I knew what I had signed up to and said that I was unlikely to complete it, even though they sponsored me anyway. Though, I do think it was more that they felt sorry for everything I had been through. I personally didn't think I was going to make it either, but the more people told me I wouldn't be able to, the more I wanted to prove them wrong. Because I had to do it, because people needed those TVs in hospital, so even if it took all day to drag myself around the course, then that's what I would do.

So, we trained solid for months, with me pushing myself more than I could ever have done before. 14 July was the day of the event. I remember arriving and feeling terrified.

Everyone looked so fit and able, and I looked like I wasn't going to make it. My outfit wasn't even right. Then I thought, *what am I doing? I shouldn't be here*. However, I couldn't drop out.

We got stuck in. It was so hard. I had to push myself to get round. I was absolutely terrified of deep water or being submerged in water. One of the first obstacles was water-based, requiring you to fully submerge. It was a skip filled with ice and you had to go in, go under tyres and come out the other side.

I remember doing it and not being able to submerge, no matter what I did. I started to panic and cry. I remember a guy standing on the side telling me I could do it, that when I was under water to feel for his hand, and he would guide me out the other side. I was able to do this and come out the other side. Whilst I was shaky as hell afterwards, I felt so proud to have done something I hated so much. Though I vowed never to experience that again.

Getting around that course with Natalie was such a crazy experience. I cried; I laughed; there were moments I wanted to quit, but we got round because everyone on the course worked as a team. It was so hard, the hardest thing I had ever done. When I crossed the finish line thirteen miles later, battered and bruised, I can't tell you how proud I felt. Actually, it was one of the proudest moments of my life as I did something I thought I couldn't do but, more importantly, I had pushed myself around that course to support others. I raised enough to fund seven TVs from that challenge, which was pretty awesome. I knew I needed to get another seven, and I was determined I was going to get that money so I could get them the following year.

That September I was turning thirty. The last half of my twenties weren't what I had imagined. Never would I have expected to experience what I had. Everything that happened changed me as a person and life felt completely different. I had lost a lot of people I had loved. I had lost friends and gained new ones. I got into debt to buy stuff to impress people I didn't care about, but when my house flooded, I lost it all anyway. I took on a whole new appreciation and meaning for life. It just shows you – you can't map out your life to the letter as you just don't know what will happen.

That August I went to Ibiza, a place that I had wanted to go forever, and I had the best weekend of my life. One of my friends said, "If you do anything, go and watch the sunset at Café Mambo – it's a very magical moment." I couldn't at the time see how something as simple as that could be special, but I was wrong.

I remember sitting there watching the sunset. With the sunset, music playing and everyone sitting watching, I thought about everything that had happened to us, about life, and it was in that moment I realised that it was time for change for me and I wanted to do something to help others. It's crazy how you can get all that from a sunset, but I did. From that moment, I knew something special was going to happen, even though I didn't know what it was.

2015

The hospital visits and trips continued. Work was work; life was life. The fundraising had spurred me on and given me a purpose, knowing I was doing something good to help others, but after that, life felt flat and I just got back into the day-to-day routine. I just felt like I was drifting along.

I decided I would start 2015 by taking on another challenge to get the remaining seven TVs that were needed for the hospital ward. I asked my friend Natalie, "Do you fancy doing another challenge as we ticked off Tough Mudder?" I decided to do some research and find a challenge that was even tougher than the last one. That's when I came across Rat Race Dirty Weekend – twenty miles, two hundred obstacles. Natalie luckily said yes; between us we decided that, whilst it sounded hard, it couldn't be that hard. We didn't even bother to look into it on that basis. In a way, that's a good thing as if I realised what it was really like, I don't think I would have even showed up.

I remember that day a few months later – we were there at the start line, that was when the realisation hit of what we had signed up for, and we just looked at each other like *what the hell are we doing?*

I had received sponsorship so there was the expectation for me to now deliver. I had no choice but to crack on. It was so hard. My knee was in agony by mile five and I had no clue why, but I didn't stop, even though the further the distance got, the more painful it became. Randomly, Natalie seemed to be having the same problem too.

We tried to lift each other's spirits and push each other along. Some parts it was easy to make a joke and keep each other going; other times I was in a foul mood because I didn't want to be there.

There was a get-out at the halfway point – even though both of us were thinking, *shall we quit?* neither of us wanted to be the one to say it. To be fair, I could have quit there and then. No one would be the wiser. However, my driving force was that these TVs were going to make a difference to someone else's life, and not just one person but multiple people who came through that ward. That reminder was enough for me to keep going and push me every mile until the finish line.

I crossed the finish line looking a state. I was cold, muddy, smelt bad and couldn't stop shaking. Not my finest hour, but I did it and got enough money to raise the remaining amount for the TVs. For me, that was the best feeling ever.

Once the money was dropped off at the hospital, it felt good. Mission accomplished. I had done what I set out to do. This was to make a difference, and I knew the TVs would.

In the process, I found that I actually liked obstacle running and I was a lot stronger than I thought, physically and mentally. I started to do more of these races and started to find I was actually enjoying myself. As a person who hated sports at school, I completely surprised myself.

Having raised two sums of money, I realised now that helping others was something I wanted to do. However, if I was going to continue to raise money, it needed to be attached to something that had meaning. What did people actually need?

I decided I was going to use this newfound love for running to raise money for other things to help adult cancer patients in hospital, but it was figuring out what.

My life seemed to have calmed down from all the pain and loss that we had experienced in the last five years. It felt easier and a little bit better. The hospital visits for Janice slowed down and seemed, for the first time in years, to be getting better.

She was stronger than she had been in years, and life felt a bit more in control. It was nice to have some calm.

For the first time, it gave me time to reflect about life and what I wanted to do with it.

Over the next few months, as we headed to the end of 2015, it was a frequent conversation I not only had with myself but also with Lee. We were both thinking about what the two of us could do to help others who were going through cancer or were experiencing the situations that we had found really tough. It only felt right that we do something to give back to those people so that no one felt the way that we did.

Lee and I continued to have the conversation over and over about wanting to do something to help others. We couldn't think of what organisation we would like to support so we thought about creating something of our own. A charity that would cheer people up as they were going through cancer treatment. The more we spoke about it, the more we wanted to create something that could support adult cancer patients through their treatment.

We reflected back to what we witnessed and experienced during our endless hospital visits. When we would go in and visit Janice, we would go to the shop and buy things for people. Just simple things– sweets, a newspaper, a puzzle book. We thought about how people were always happy to receive them, how we had the most amazing conversations and how the act of giving something so small made a difference. We knew our concept of a charity would work around that whole idea of giving a gift to make someone smile.

We kept debating what this gift would be and how the person would get it, especially now we weren't visiting the ward. We thought as they knew us, hopefully they could let us in.

It was just a case of figuring out how we were going to do it and make it work.

Our initial idea was that a patient on the ward could fill in a slip about what item they wanted or needed, which they could put in a box at reception. They could choose an item they wanted or needed up to the value of £20. We could collect the slips once a week, go buy the items and bring them back to the person on the ward.

In our mind, we had convinced ourselves this would work. We didn't take any guidance from anyone; we didn't ask anyone if they thought it was a good idea or did the hospital actually want this.

We kept toying with names, trying to outdo each other. Then one day, Lee said,

"How about The Lewis Foundation?" It felt right, we went with that and got the application off. We waited to see what would happen.

2016

We had no clue if our application to the charity commission was going to be approved. We weren't sure if the information included in the application was right or if we had given them what they needed to assure them we were genuine. It was just a waiting game to see if they would say yes.

2016 was a year when I started to really reflect on my own life, how I was living it and what I in fact wanted. I decided I wanted to make some changes. The last five years had made me realise life was far too short to be doing something that didn't make me feel happy. One area that I had started to become unhappy with was my day job.

I had been at my job for eight years. I was getting frustrated at not having a work/life balance, which this period made me realise how important that was.

Everyone said that once you got this job, you would be there for life until you retired, and you would never leave. When completing the staff survey that year, it asked me how soon I wanted to leave. The fact that I said as soon as possible said it all. I knew I had to do something about it.

I decided to apply for the job I had originally always wanted when I said I wanted to practise law. That job was to work at the Crown Prosecution Service in London as a prosecutor. It would be a job where I could prepare the cases for the hearings and trial, with the hours being controllable and having the ability to work from home. Plus, I would be researching law and preparing cases, which was something that I would love – I would be in my element.

I remember travelling down to London for the interview and hoping I would be good enough. I thought about all those times I used to travel down for work experience, but now I was potentially going to be travelling down to actually do a job I wanted to do. It made me realise how far I had come.

The interview seemed to be going amazing, with the written assignment and presentation part going well. Then, when it came to the questions, it all seemed to be going fine until they asked me a question and my mind went blank. There wasn't anything there and I couldn't think of a word to say.

I asked if I could come back to it and tried to redeem myself but totally thought I messed it up. I was absolutely gutted with myself. I left feeling crap and going home thinking I had messed up my one opportunity to do something that I really wanted to.

Therefore, I was shocked when they rang me the next day to say I was successful. I couldn't believe it. Whilst I was excited and happy, I was so scared about telling my employer. I was one of those people who didn't like to say anything for fear of letting people down or worrying about what people thought. However, I knew I was going to have to say it because I wasn't happy anymore and I knew for me it was the right thing to do.

However, when I did tell my employer I was leaving, they were shocked. They tried to persuade me to stay. Everyone was saying I was making a mistake and I was going to regret it. There is nothing harder than trying to stand your ground and not waver when everyone is telling you that you shouldn't be doing something.

I handed in my notice knowing that I would be leaving my safety blanket in August.

* * *

The months went by as we were waiting for the Charity Commission to give us permission to become an official charity; that date came on 7 April 2016.

I remember coming home from work that day and seeing the email to say that The Lewis Foundation was now an officially registered charity.

I remember telling Lee and we couldn't believe that they actually thought it was a good idea that could work. I think that surprised us most of all.

Even though I was excited by it, I was so nervous and worried about what others would think about us. Would they think it was stupid? How was what we were doing going to make a difference? Why were we bothering or why did we even care?

I did care a lot about what people thought and those thoughts did put a dampener on how I felt about doing something that was important and really mattered to me.

The more we talked about it, the more the reality set in as we sat down and discussed how we were going to officially launch this. We had no funds, so we couldn't buy anything that we wanted to. Then we realised we had not asked the hospital whether this was in fact OK. Suppose we asked to start, and they totally rejected our idea? All we had was a name and a charity status; it felt like we had already failed, and we hadn't even started yet.

The thing was, we had no clue what we needed to do or how. We just knew we wanted to help others. That was our sole aim.

We did what we originally should have done, which was contact our local Northampton hospital and ask for a meeting to check if we could actually do this. We prayed they would let us, otherwise everything else had been a complete waste of time.

Luckily, they were receptive and supportive to what we had to say. However, the concept of what we wanted to achieve had to be tweaked to make it workable.

They said, "The suggestion of the slip may prove tricky. Suppose someone ordered something but by time you came in they'd already gone home, which meant you would be stuck with an item and no one to give it to. You might find you struggle to get an item that someone needs and then you would have to keep going back and forth to find it or source something else. Realistically, it wouldn't work, it's too complicated and needs to be simplified."

Thinking back to what we used to do, which was go to the hospital, go to the shop, get people items and allow people to pick what item they would like, it made total sense to do this but packaged up as a gift in a nice way. That's when we knew what we needed to do.

We wanted the gifts branded, nice and decent, so it was actually a gift. A nice treat, a surprise. There would be no donations or money given for it; we believed the kindness would pay itself back at a later date in some other way.

We wanted people to see that there could be genuine kindness and that you could give something without expecting anything back in return.

It would be something people would want and would look forward to. I remember when people used to come round the ward and, all of a sudden, I would notice my mother-in-law shut her eyes and pretend she was asleep. She didn't want to chat about something she didn't want or consider buying something she didn't need.

We didn't want people to do that when we visited; we wanted them to be happy to see us. It was decided that our charity having a range of gifts for people to pick from was what we were going to do.

Now we just needed the money and the products to be able to make it happen.

I wrote to everyone and anyone to see if they would donate products for our gift packs. I told them our story in the letters, writing each one out by hand which took me forever.

I put them in the brightest envelopes so people didn't think it was a bill or junk – fun mail!

I wrote to people who I never dreamed would have written back – *BBC Magazine*, Yorkshire Tea and *Puzzler*. The thing is, they did write back, and they were saying they would be more than happy to support and make a donation. We were blown away as we were expecting them to say no. It actually blew me away that people would do that – it was amazing.

Whilst we tried to get it off the ground, I had kept it fairly quiet amongst people I knew that we had set up a charity. I don't know why, but I was kind of embarrassed because I didn't think people would get it. The thing was, I needed the publicity to get it off the ground, so I needed to make people aware. I decided the best way was via the *Chronicle & Echo*, which was our local paper.

There was a reporter at work, who I asked to cover our charity set-up, and he did. We needed the publicity and support, yet we didn't want anyone to know. It went into our local newspaper *Chronicle and Echo* – 'local couple set up a charity', with a picture of Lee and me on my thirtieth totally over the top and dressed up. It wasn't like we had any charity-related photos, outfits or pictures of what we were doing. It didn't at all match what we were trying to share, but people who knew us spotted it and then the word got out.

Then everyone started talking about it. Some people were brilliant, totally supportive. A lot of people didn't get it, and some were taking the mick out of it, which was hard and upsetting. For some reason, I cared more about the ones who didn't get it than the ones who did. That stopped me from telling people about the charity because of certain people's reactions – they made me feel embarrassed.

It's amazing how the people you thought would support you don't. Yet, people who didn't really know you or you weren't that close to did.

Thanks to donations of gift items from companies, and fundraising where we could, we were ready to make our first delivery of gifts in May 2016.

We went out and got some really nice white gift packs, those nice paper ones that you get when you actually receive a gift. Even though we could have got bags cheaper, we didn't think a brown paper bag was the look we were going for. We used our £35 Canon printer to make up a label to put on the bag. It had our logo and listed all the contents that were in the bag. Then, we used Pritt Stick to glue the label on.

Getting the remainder of the items we needed consisted of going to Poundland and the supermarkets, which was to supplement what we didn't get donated by businesses. We created a few different packs – overnight pack with toiletries and underwear, magazines, books, colouring books, radios, etc. Things that we had observed during our time in hospital that could make people feel better. We packaged them all up ready for delivery. Eighty gifts ready to go.

We had nothing to store them in to take them to the hospital. We asked our friend Keith if he had a really big cardboard box that would be big enough to put all the gifts in. He got us a furniture cardboard box, which was perfect even if it was huge. We put all the gift packs inside and took them to the hospital for our first delivery.

The box of gifts took over the little bit of space the nurses had. It was such an amazing feeling to have this idea that we could now physically see before us. However, what the long-term plan was, we couldn't tell you. We would just keep doing what we wanted to do, which was to help people.

The plan was that we would drop these gifts off on a monthly basis, and the nurses would hand out the gifts to patients for us. In the meantime, we would continue to contact companies and fundraise where we could so we could ensure that we would get gifts to the hospital each and every month. It made life a bit more exciting, rather than just going to work and coming home to just veg out in front of the TV, watching soap after soap.

The hardest part about this was getting support from people outside our immediate family, friends and colleagues to understand what we wanted to do and what we were trying to achieve. I get why as, if a stranger had asked me to buy someone a gift who I didn't know to cheer them up, I have to admit I would have thought it was weird and said no. So, I totally got it, but it still didn't stop that frustrating feeling that we just needed someone to give us a break.

The key problem was no one really knew who we were and couldn't understand why we wanted to give out gifts for free. As a result, we were constantly turned down for support.

We got turned away by so many people. The constant question was: how is a gift going to help someone?

No amount of explanation could persuade people we were telling the truth and that it did help. At the time, we hadn't built up a big enough reputation for the recipients of our gifts to speak on our behalf, so we had no feedback to support the impact of our work.

If anything, we saw it as a challenge; we would keep persisting and doing what we needed to do – it would pay off at some point in the future. This did mean we leaned heavily on family and friends. It was thanks to friends and work colleagues who started to do their own fundraising to support us, raising a couple of hundred here and there, that we were able to make our deliveries each month.

I decided to get back to running to raise money and, along with two of my work friends, signed up to do 5k mud run on 4 June 2016 in Abington Park in Northampton. We decided to get T-shirts printed with our logo on, as I realised you always saw people running for charities with charity tops on and it would help to get the word out there.

No one had a clue who we were, with people constantly asking, "What is The Lewis Foundation?" However, I didn't see it as a bad thing as it would at least give me a chance to explain. Hopefully, drum up some more awareness and support.

We ran, took loads of pictures and were able to raise £200; all donations at that time helped to enable us to do our work.

That summer, I closed the chapter on my job as a legal adviser and, leaving that final day, I knew it was the right thing to do. However, I would be forever grateful for the support some of my colleagues had given me, not only in my personal life but also helping me with getting the charity off the ground. In September, my fresh start began at the Crown Prosecution Service and I felt I had finally reached where I should be.

* * *

We were six months in now to dropping off gifts each month to the hospital; we had now got into a routine that seemed to be working well. As the months went on, we had started to get people contacting us directly for our gift packs who were on the ward in the hospital.

They wanted a pack, but they didn't want to disturb the nurses. We appreciated the nurses were giving out our packs whenever they could, and having spent so much time on that ward, we knew how busy they were.

We were finding we were going in to give someone a pack and then ending up having a chat. Then, before we knew it, we were giving out our packs to other people on the ward. It wasn't long before we were doing a ward visiting round. What we could then see with our own eyes was that our work was making a difference to people, and seeing it first-hand confirmed why we were doing this in the first place.

As the requests kept coming from patients requesting a pack, we thought maybe we should go in and do a ward visit every week. We were pretty much doing that anyway. We could go in, do a visit, hand out some gifts, then people would know we were coming. We could also chat to people whilst we were there, something people seemed to enjoy.

We raised our idea with the hospital, who were absolutely fine with this and said it would be a nice thing to do for the patients.

We were both excited but also nervous about going onto the ward. The nerves being because we would be doing our hospital visits in a more official capacity.

We picked Friday night because it was something to look forward to at the end of the week. I know how glad I was for the end of the week and how I looked forward to a Friday finish at work. As in hospital every day blurs into one, with no day to look forward to other than going home. Patients never really knew what day they were going home.

Getting ready to do official ward visits meant that we needed to get prepared. We purchased some tubs so we could bring a selection of each gift with us so that there was a choice and hopefully everyone would then get the gift they wanted. We also needed something to wheel the tubs around the ward on, so Lee sourced a sack barrow to do this. Lee also created this gift menu for people to look at and select what they would like. There were eight gifts on there, and it stated what you would get inside each gift, with an accompanying picture of the contents.

It was all a learning curve as we had never done this before, and we had no one we could go to for advice as to whether this would work or was the right thing to do. It was literally learning as you go.

The first time Lee and I went onto the ward on a Friday evening, we were so nervous about handing out the packs. Then, each of us was encouraging the other to go into a room or a bay first to hand out the gifts, seeing who would be the one brave enough to go in first. The nurses watching us found it hilarious. I actually don't know what was wrong with us, but we gave each other a pep talk and finally got stuck in with the visit. After getting over the nerves of the first few rooms, it was fine. We soon realised the hardest part wasn't talking to people but persuading them we were genuinely giving them a gift with nothing in return.

Patients were wary, understandably so. If the shoe was on the other foot, I would have been the same. People weren't sure if they took a gift whether we were going to suddenly demand money at a later date. The people who said no would observe us with others to see if there was a money exchange with the people who were willing to take the risk and accept a gift. Once satisfied we were genuine, we would then get called back to say the person had changed their mind.

Our experience on the ward made us realise that we live in a world where people are suspicious if you give them something nice for free because you genuinely want to help and not because you want something in return. Something that, in this day and age, is actually really sad. We knew it would take time and if anything, we enjoyed the challenge of changing that perception. This was something we knew was going to take time.

We continued to show up weekly and the more we did, the more people started to get to know and trust us.

The early days were still really hard work because we were just trying to find our feet. Learn what to say, how to act or what to do. We knew we had the ability to communicate and listen, which was so important for what we were doing. However, it was the intimacy of the work we were doing that was the learning curve.

When you thought about it, you were going into someone's private space, effectively their bedroom. They were in their bed, in their pyjamas or hospital gown and hooked up to some sort of machine – yet they were trusting you to go in that space. They trusted you enough to share information about themselves – who they were, what they liked, stories about them and their families, their worries and concerns. Information they really didn't have to share with you.

It made us realise this was more than just giving a gift, and there were so many hurdles you had to jump through from the minute you knocked on that person's door.

It was knowing how to handle the situation when you opened the door to a private room or walked up to someone's space in a bay, knowing within a split second what to do next.

I learnt once that how you react is so important to how you make the other person feel. A lady I had got to know over a couple of months took a turn. I was used to seeing her happy and smiling face, excited for her visits. One day, I opened her door and she looked like she was about to die, and I was shocked. She asked me to leave her a gift on the side. I shut the door and left. The next week she was sitting up and was much better. She said to me, "I'm so sorry, I didn't mean to scare you." That was a lesson learnt on how I needed to present myself because by looking scared, I had also scared her. I hadn't even realised I had given this away.

As I said, every week, I learnt something new every ward visit I made so that, over time, I got more confident in myself during these visits.

Outside the hospital, it was becoming apparent how much work a charity required, something that no one ever speaks about. You see the day-to-day project work but never behind the scenes.

There was so much more to learn about the charity. The boring stuff, as I would call it. Things such as policies, training, preparing accounts. With no one to turn to other than each other, we just tried our best to make it work and hoped not to fail. Every day was a school day, that's for sure.

2017

Whilst we tried to figure out how to run a charity, one thing that was becoming more apparent was that money was becoming an issue.

I remember opening up our charity bank statement in February 2017 and we only had £107 left. It shocked me, and when I told Lee, it shocked him as well. Whilst every month had been tough, I don't think we fully appreciated what position we had been reaching financially each month.

We were scared as we knew we were running out of money, and we didn't really know what we were going to do to overcome it. I wasn't sure how we would make it past March at this stage. If we had no money, that would be it, the end. Game over. We wouldn't have made it a year.

I felt like we had failed if we decided to stop, and Lee felt the same as me. We had worked too hard to let this fail.

That's why stopping was never an option for us, and we would always find a way to continue no matter what. We weren't sure how we were going to make it work but we would find a way. We knew it was time to extend beyond just seeking support from our friends, family and colleagues.

We also knew we hadn't built up a big enough reputation for people to know who we were to want to support us. We had to relook at what we were doing and create a plan of action going forward.

We realised we spent far too much money on items and that we needed to start shopping around, getting items cheaper and that some items really weren't realistic. Some of the gifts we were providing were just not necessary – dressing gowns, in hindsight, weren't something we needed to give as a gift. The gift list had somehow evolved into something completely different from what we had envisaged. To survive, we had to get back on track.

With a revised and more sensible gift list, we knew we could move forward. It was the first time we had any real plan of action, which we hoped would move us forward in the right direction. We just wanted someone who had enough funds to believe in us. Money was literally our only barrier here to making it work.

Then, two things happened that changed everything.

In February 2017, I stumbled across a tweet one evening for the Eden Project Community Camp. It was a chance to learn everything possible about how to build a community, something we desperately needed, considering the delicate financial situation we were in. This was going to take place at the Eden Project in Cornwall. I decided to apply, not really believing that we would get it, or that a charity would be what they were looking for. I just hoped they took a chance on us and that we could use it as a way to learn. I sent it off, not expecting to hear anything back.

I was surprised when I got invited for a telephone interview where more questions were asked about us and our work. I just poured out everything that had ever happened to us, our whole life story. I wasn't sure if it was a good or bad move, but I really hoped that by sharing, if anything, they would see our passion, drive and determination to make a difference. They did, as a few days later, I found out we were successful.

Whilst initially, it was just a place for one, the both of us were able to go. All we knew about the Eden Project at the time was that it was the place on the TV where we had seen those biodomes. There was no real information that came out about the event other than the fact we were going to stay on site for four days with accommodation, and we would be fed.

Once we had found out we had got in, we started to panic. What if people thought we were rubbish, we looked unprofessional or people saw us for who we were – people who wanted to help but didn't have a clue what they were doing? So, we decided to make ourselves look as professional as we could. Heading to our printer, we made sure we were kitted up with branded jackets, tops and bags. Even if we didn't know what we were doing, we were going to attempt to look the part.

A month later, we made our journey down to Cornwall. I had completely misread the time and realised en route so we were going to arrive late. The good thing was that, on arrival, someone thought we were speakers, which was great for us as we realised that we looked the part. Though, that high was quickly altered by the walk of shame we had to do in front of everyone, with the only seats available being the ones right at the front of the room; plus, we realised everyone had dressed normally.

However, hands down that's up there as one of the best weekends of my life. To be in a room with sixty different people, with a variety of different ideas, who wanted to make the world a better place. We had to bring one thing that represented us, and we brought a gift bag and then shared our story. Even though we were embarrassed about what we did in comparison to everyone else. The embarrassment being that everyone seemed to know exactly what to do and how to do it, whilst we did not. However, people were saying this was a really good thing and it was going to grow. Not that we believed them.

Yet, from that weekend we took away so many things – how to grow a community, the fact you can apply for funding (didn't even know that was a thing?!) and the power of building communities. Plus, we had so much fun – a private tour in the biodomes after dark and getting to listen to powerful inspirational speakers which made me realise we can all do something to change the world. Then we had an end of weekend party in the grounds, which was incredible.

The one thing I really learnt from that weekend was about pushing the boundaries even when you feel like you're going to fail, when people tell you no and when you feel like giving up. That was what we needed to hear when we were on the brink of having to stop: we would find a way to keep going.

That weekend fundamentally changed how we perceived everything but, more importantly, it gave us the self-belief that this idea we had could go bigger and beyond what we were doing at that time. Even though we couldn't see how we were going to get there or how we were going to even generate enough funds to get there, we knew we would find a way to make that happen. Everything changed after that weekend. We felt like maybe what we were doing really did matter and we could make a real difference to the lives of others.

And it did – we had a spring in our step as we worked really hard to cut costs and make things work. We felt we had this.

Even though money was still an issue, we felt like, this time, we could resolve it. Having been to the community camp, we now realised that we could apply for funding.

Our charity work continued, our weekly hospital visits forming part of our routine. We were meeting so many people in and out of the hospital, getting to know them beyond their cancer.

During this time, there was a guy that Lee would ask me to make up packs for on a regular basis called Mike. He would come into Lee's work and Lee, on his breaks, would go and have a drink and a chat with him. He would also give him one of the gift packs that I prepared to support him as he went through treatment. I would fill it with so many different things: puzzle books, hand creams and creams for the skin. Anything that would help him to feel a little bit better. I never met him personally, but Lee would tell me about him and how happy he was with the packs. One day, Lee had learnt through work that he had passed away. Of course, he was sad as he had got to know him. We didn't know his family or friends to contact them and pass on our sympathy.

Then, one day out of the blue, we got a letter through the post, and it was about Mike. He had left £50,000 to The Lewis Foundation to support our work. We couldn't believe it; we didn't think it was real until it was there in black and white. We were genuinely shocked that someone believed in us that much to want to support us in that way. The fact that he valued what we did so much he left a legacy to enable us to continue to help others in his memory. It was such an incredible and unexpected act of kindness.

This generous donation, together with what we had learnt from the Eden Project, changed everything for us. Our financial worry had gone, which meant we didn't have to stop. We realised it meant we could help even more people, and that's just what we did.

After that, we approached BMI Three Shires Hospital, a private hospital in Northampton.

Then we started with our packs on oncology for day patients at Northampton General Hospital. We found the more we gave, the more people got to know who we were and started to spread the word about what we did.

What really made people regard us as credible was when we won Sainsbury's Charity of the Year for our local Northampton store. We so desperately wanted to win so that people could take us seriously. It shouldn't have to be that way, but I knew we would have to persuade people we were decent and genuine.

We were up against two other charities and it was based on who got the most votes. We pushed it hard online and in person. We were complete underdogs – family, friends and patients all rallied around supporting us.

When we found out we had won it was the best feeling ever. People who didn't believe in us started to.

We also got featured in *Take A Break* about our work, which, for us to be featured in a national publication, was a big deal, especially as such a new charity. That publicity worked, with people in our community who hadn't spoken to us before or shown much interest coming up to us and saying they'd seen us in the magazine.

However, with exposure brought people who wanted to take advantage, a lesson we learnt about how naïve we really were. People knew we were desperate to get publicity and support as we really wanted this to work.

A guy got in contact with us to say he was doing a Comic Con race and wanted to choose us as the chosen charity. It was in Birmingham, so to be fair, alarm bells should have rung at this stage. However, we were just so happy someone wanted to support us. We googled the event. There was lots of promotion going on. It all seemed legitimate and above board.

The suggestion was that we get a team together that could run at the race and promote what we do. We would get a discount for this, and we would get a donation from every entry. It all sounded too good to be true, and that's because it was.

The closer it got, the more something didn't feel quite right about the event and about him as the organiser. He kept up the pretence, but I still couldn't shake it. I remember saying to my friend I wasn't sure if I want to go, and she said, "Don't then." So, I told the people who said they would do it that we wouldn't be going. We decided to pull out. If he was going to raise money from entries, we would get it sent after.

However, the weekend of the race, it soon became apparent that the race didn't exist. Questions started to be asked and angry comments were posted via social media.

People had turned up and there was nothing there. It was a scam and he had taken people's money. He had disappeared, along with all methods of contact, and we were the only people whose details were contactable on his website. People started to contact us. Luckily, they were understanding, but I wasn't only mortified, I also felt humiliated and extremely upset. I felt stupid for not knowing and I hated being taken advantage of when all we were trying to do was something nice.

Then I was contacted by the local radio there to come on air and give our side of the story, and even though I had done nothing wrong, I felt so bad for those people. The last thing I wanted to do was go on air and say I hadn't realised I had been scammed. Then I would have to take the grilling and pray no one doubted that we had no knowledge of this.

We never heard from him again. Number dead, Facebook blocked. However, afterwards, I learnt this wasn't the first time he had done this. However, for us it was a major lesson in making sure you get all the information, ask questions and know who to trust.

We got back on our feet after this and kept going.

Our hospital visits and direct interactions with people meant we were learning about the worries, the struggles and support patients needed. What we identified was the problems that people said they were facing were similar. They were the same problems my mother-in-law used to mention when she was going through cancer. Things such as, 'my nails are brittle', 'why has my skin changed?', 'how do I stop thinking about cancer?' etc. There were so many questions and concerns for patients that we felt we had to create something that would help to alleviate these problems but also bring people together.

We decided to put on a 'pamper day' event for patients. It was a day that would be completely free, where we could address all the queries and concerns that people had. Get it out of their heads and addressed. Connect with other people going through what they were, which would hopefully create some connections that lasted beyond the event.

For us it was important to take it out of the clinical setting of a hospital, a place where people spent so much time following a cancer diagnosis. It was a place that people wanted to avoid unless they specifically had to be there for cancer treatment.

We chose a nice hotel, a place you could go to if you wanted to do something special. It would help to create a change of scene from the hospital setting and not be so clinical. The hardest part then became convincing people that this day would be free because they just didn't get why we wanted to do that. It took a lot of persuasion to convince people there were going to be no hidden costs, there wasn't a secret agenda and that we just wanted to help.

I knew with this event, Lee wouldn't be able to be there with me on the day and I would be on my own, something which terrified me as, at least when Lee was there with me, even if we had no clue what we were doing, we could give each other a pep talk, encouraging the other to get on with it. However, the driving factor here was that I had to get on with it. I had to make it work because if we were asking patients to come along to a day like this, then I needed to ensure that the day was of some value to them.

The day went great. We got to meet amazing people who were able to take a lot of value from what was shared. There were talks around skincare, nail loss, mental health and also people got to have treatments. It was so good to hear people say that the day helped to alleviate their worries and concerns that they had. It had helped to answer their questions and it was wonderful to see people connecting together.

For the rest of the year, we were getting into a good routine with packing and getting the gifts handed out at the hospital. We were becoming more comfortable and were enjoying it. As it approached Christmas time, this year we thought we wanted to do something special for people.

A family friend got in contact with us and wanted to do something to help others in memory of her father. A Christmas fete was organised to raise funds and awareness of the work we do in our local working men's club, which enabled us to raise £732. It was decided that we would put this towards making people feel special at Christmas.

We decided to surprise people with a Christmas hamper, which we could fill with festive food and drink goodies. People could nominate a family member or friend to receive a hamper from us. It would be delivered to their door as a surprise in the lead-up to Christmas.

The hardest part was getting people to nominate as they couldn't understand why we wanted to give away a hamper for free. We begged people to nominate, asking people we knew to put someone forward. In the end, we got seventeen nominations, which I'm not sure how we managed to achieve given the difficulty we had persuading people to nominate.

Nationwide head office in Northampton got involved in packing and wrapping the hampers to make them look beautiful as, between Lee and me, our wrapping attempts were shocking.

It was an incredible experience handing out these hampers. People were genuinely shocked they were receiving them. We were invited into people's homes to have a drink with them, a chat and to give them a better understanding of what we did and why.

Just hearing the stories of how it made a difference was enough to make doing this totally worth it. People would be able to now enjoy items they didn't think they would be able to afford to buy; it had taken people's minds off endless bad news, and the list went on. We completely underestimated how much positivity could come from doing this. Seventeen took three weeks because of the length of time we spent with people. However, those moments were so special and worth it as we could see the real difference it was going to make, and we said it was something we would definitely do every year.

On Christmas morning, we decided to go and hand gifts out on Talbot Butler Ward at Northampton General Hospital, something I would never have dreamed of doing before. Christmas morning usually involved waking up, cracking open the bubbly and chocolates and being on your way by lunchtime. However, we have never forgotten that Christmas Day we spent in Leicester Royal Infirmary, even though that happened a while ago . So, we put on some festive wear and made our way to the ward, armed with gift boxes with a £20 voucher and festive goodies. We went around the ward handing out gifts and chatting to people. The Salvation Army brass band played Christmas tunes on the ward, and it was beautiful. It took an hour that day to go round the ward visiting people, an hour that, after I left, I can't explain how it made me feel, but I felt that by giving that hour, it embodied the meaning of Christmas. Then I was back home enjoying our Christmas Day, in the hope that our visit had been one thing that had made the day a bit better for someone else. It was the best present I could ask for.

Before we knew it, it was the end of 2017, and it was amazing how so much had been crammed in within the space of a year. It was amazing to see how that year we had given away 3,325 gift packs, more than we could ever have imagined. It felt like it was the beginning of the next chapter of our adventure, and it really was, because in the next two years, the charity really took off in a way that none of us could have ever expected.

2018

The charity in 2018 started in full swing – gifts were going out and the support was growing. Donations were flowing in – money and gift items. We were running the charity from our home, which was slowly starting to feel more and more like a warehouse each week. Boxes were being sent to us by companies, who didn't realise we were running this from our home address. This, as a result, always left the delivery drivers puzzled – they would turn up to our house and be surprised. Once they got over it, the delivery would be unloaded into our hallway, with us left to figure out how we were going to accommodate it.

What we couldn't get through product donations, we had to hit the shops for. We were literally clearing the shelves. Even the shops were getting sick of us. The dirty looks when they saw us coming. The constant questions – 'Why do you need so much?', 'What are you doing with all this stuff?' To be honest, we were getting sick and tired of having to justify ourselves when we were simply trying to do something to help others. During one purchase of a hundred pair of socks, Lee pretended that he was using them to make puppets for a puppet show. Followed by a demo. They soon shut up and never asked questions again.

Then, one day, we were sharing our difficulties with the shops with a friend and then the suggestion, 'Have you thought about a wholesaler?' a thought that hadn't even crossed our minds. As soon as we signed up, it made the process so much easier and stress-free.

Over the months, our house was slowly getting out of control and becoming unliveable.

We literally had no space to even live in. Every room was filled with items because we had nowhere to put them. Everywhere you looked, there were gifts. It got to the stage where you had to move boxes to see the TV and Lee and I could no longer cross paths in the house, waiting for the other person to go first. Reminding ourselves what we learnt from Eden about funding, we set about applying for the first time for some funding, working out what was a priority that we needed.

We knew storage space couldn't be more urgent for us and we needed a printer. Our canon printer was barely hanging on; I'm not sure how it was surviving, but it was. However, at the rate it was going, it wasn't going to hold out much longer.

Thank God the grants we applied for with the National Lottery for £10,000 and the Northamptonshire Community Foundation for £3,000 were successful. When we were told we would receive both, the tears of relief were unreal.

We were able to upgrade our printer to something more manageable and better quality than what we were using. When we saw the difference in print quality between the two, we couldn't believe it. We cringed so badly at how poor the other ones looked. You had to laugh but whilst they hadn't been perfect, they had done the job and they had helped to make a difference. Though, we couldn't stop laughing at how bad it was.

The funding meant that we could also start to move items out of our home so we could have a home again. We got a small, garage-size storage room to start putting things in to try and reclaim our home.

The patients who were receiving our packs were doing an amazing job of spreading awareness about what we did, which meant more people were hearing about our work, and this was leading to further support. The people who were receiving our packs were absolutely amazing at doing this. The feedback of how it was helping to make a real difference was driving us on to want to do even more. Whilst we knew when we set it up that it would make a difference, we just didn't realise how much of a difference it would make, and the wonderful thing was that the patients were doing things to help us to support others in their position.

One special moment was when a family decided to fundraise to help support us by doing a head shave. However, what made it different was the fact that three sisters were going to shave off their hair in support of their sister who was going through cancer treatment. I was really moved witnessing that because it wasn't a case of simply doing a head shave to raise money; that was the by-product. The real drive behind it was to support their loved one so that they knew they weren't alone, even if it must have been scary for them to shave off their hair. That moment when they all stood together after everyone's hair had gone, and the emotion that was being shared between them, will stay with me forever. It was moments like these which made the work we were doing have meaning and fulfilled my sense of purpose.

When we were going about doing our everyday charity work, we were just doing it, and it was never about what we would get in return. It was just about doing something to make someone else feel that little bit better. We were contacted by BP to ask if we would be their charity of the year in their stores in Northamptonshire and on the M1, which was major for us and we couldn't believe they would want to support us. We weren't even sure of how they knew who we were.

We remember going in to meet the manager, who looked vaguely familiar, but I couldn't place at all where from. She started talking about supporting us before telling us the reason why. I had spoken to her friend in Talbot Butler Ward before she died. I had come in and spoken to her, given her time, made eye contact, basically had a normal human conversation. It touched her that I would just speak to her normally. I remember the conversation well and I realised I had remembered the friend in the corner too. For me, I was doing nothing out of the ordinary other than speaking from human to human. Yet, I was doing something without realising the significance of its impact.

When people weren't raising money, they were putting us forward for awards and nominating us to thank us for helping them.

Our first ever award came in the form of the Northampton Heart of the Community Awards, which was a lovely award where the nominations were read out about us. We often don't think about what we do, we just do it. To hear how it made someone feel touched us.

That summer, we found out we were up for our first National awards – the National New Business Awards Not for Profit of the Year – in London. It fell on the day we were due to start the Three Peaks Challenge.

So, we decided we would go to the awards, then get a train up to the Lake District to join everyone for peaks two and three. We were extremely nervous about the award; we felt totally out of our depth. This was especially true when we arrived and just felt like small fish in a big pond. We never expected to win, and no one had a clue who we were. But we were somehow ended as runners-up and it was an amazing feeling which helped with getting publicity and support for our work. Therefore, for us it was an evening to celebrate. Though, I regret celebrating to the extent I did because the next day, heading up on the train to the Lake District from London, was absolute torture with a hangover. In addition to the fact that weekend proved to be the hottest weekend to do the Three Peaks. However, we were able to do two out of the three peaks, raise money for charity and we had the clearest view I had ever seen at the top of Snowdon in my life.

* * *

Amazing people seemed to continue to appear in our lives to help us after we helped them in some way. Tracy reached out after we supported one of her family members and offered to help us with our marketing. However, it became more than that. She genuinely cared about our physical/mental well-being, which, even if someone had been concerned, no one ever said it to our faces. Yet, Tracy did.

Our marketing was non-existent and having never done social media before, we weren't really putting things out there which helped to raise awareness and get support for the work we were doing. Tracy came in and told us straight and, to be honest, someone needed to. We needed to look after ourselves; we needed to reclaim our home back; and she helped us realise that this wasn't a hobby. We were running a proper charity. There weren't a lot of people we would have taken that from, but she genuinely cared and had our best interests at heart. We were so grateful as she helped us go from seeing the charity as a hobby we do in our spare time to running it professionally.

We were packing the gifts in our home with our small team of volunteers. The number of gifts were starting to increase which meant it was becoming more difficult to pack them in our homes. By the time we had the volunteers and the packs in our home, there was nowhere to move. We had so many offers from people wanting to help. However, we couldn't accept it because not only wasn't there space in our home but we also wanted to retain our privacy. We didn't know what to do. Then, Tracy suggested finding a location outside our home to pack. That way, we could have more people there, whilst maintaining our privacy. This would also stop our home getting wrecked.

We made enquiries with our local community centre and asked if we could use the space to pack and they gave us a space so we could. It was the strangest experience for us, taking the packing out of our home. It was finally another step to it feeling less like a hobby and more like something that was real. However, for us to get organised and get a clear process in place was so difficult, and we knew that was due to not having enough hours in the day to do what we had to do to get it correct. Things were always missing, and we couldn't just nip upstairs like before and get them. Items didn't arrive in time, or we had ordered them too late, which meant we didn't have them in time for the packing session. So, it was kind of stressful and chaotic. We wanted so badly to be organised, but it was so hard as we were limited with time and were always learning as we went. I dread to think what people thought of us in the early days as I can fully imagine from an outside perspective it looked shambolic. I just felt so embarrassed, to the point I didn't even want to be there.

It was great having people wanting to volunteer. However, it spiralled out of control. More and more people kept turning up, to the point where we were losing control of our own sessions. As we would always miss items after a packing session, it would involve Lee and me trying to sort out the things that were missed. This had to be done after the packing session, which meant late nights and the knock-on effect of that was being tired the next day. Even though the packs went out, the process of getting the packs ready was eventful. We couldn't seem to get it right which, for someone who liked to get things right, was utterly frustrating.

Even though on the surface, it looked like we knew what we were doing, it was all learning as we went and seeing what would happen. We didn't know what we were doing, though we never let on that that was the case. Whilst we learnt and tried to figure out what we could, one thing we were certain of was that we could give our time to people; we were good at talking and listening to people. Even if we couldn't do anything else, we could do that right.

That year, the Eden Project came to visit us as part of their Big Walk. We were able to show them what we did at the hospitals, and they came round as we handed out our gift packs to patients. For us, it was crazy that the year before we had been sharing a pretty new thing about what we were doing and what we wanted to achieve and now they wanted to come and see us in action. Never did we imagine they would want to come and visit us, so it felt really special that they wanted to stay connected. It was a big deal for us to have them follow our journey and continue to support our work.

* * *

I had learnt four of the TVs I had fundraised for a few years back were no longer working as patients had contacted us because they didn't have TV to watch and asked if we could help. It had been a while since I had committed to fundraising. I decided to do the Yorkshire Three Peaks because I had seen it advertised, not really realising how hard it would be, especially when I decided to do it solo.

Everyone was saying, "Do you realise how hard it is? Is it safe to go alone?" If anything, I was also looking forward to some me time, something over the last year I hadn't really had, and some thinking time too, to clear my head. Everything with the charity was always so manic and going at a million miles an hour.

I took myself off, booked into a hotel and was ready to start the next day early in the morning. Oh my god was it hard and by the last peak, I was really struggling. However, what kept me going up the final peak was teaming up with another guy who was going solo and spurring each other on so we didn't give up. It was an amazing achievement, and when I finished nine hours later, my head was the clearest it had been in years; I had raised £600. This was enough to buy what I needed, and I was ready to get back on it.

We were able to source four large TVs which we brought down to the ward. Everyone was so excited, the staff and patients ready in time for the world cup. As soon as we arrived, they were ready and waiting for them to be installed. I will never forget the guy who was absolutely buzzing as he was now going to be able to watch the world cup. Moments like that make all the crazy things I do to fundraise worth it.

Shortly after this, it was that time of year when we would go through another nomination process for Sainsbury's Charity of the Year, which we weren't sure if we were going to win.

We saw the benefit that one year brought: funds, credibility and additional support. We knew we could only have a maximum of two years, so we wanted to make sure we got those two full years' worth of support. This was giving us more time to push out awareness and support for what we did. We worked really hard to get as many votes as we possibly could. We didn't want to lose it, and our efforts paid off. So, when we did win for a second year in a row it was a big deal for us.

The charity was getting busier, and life was getting more chaotic. I was starting to feel like I was struggling to keep a grip on everything I had to, which was extremely difficult for me as I'm person that likes to be in control; this left me feeling anxious. The knock-on effect was that my organisational skills were going out the window as I couldn't keep up. Our timekeeping became poor because we were always trying to cram so many things in, which meant that we were always late. Even for things that were really important we were late.

An example of this is when we were due to begin a new partnership with a hospital we had always wanted to work with, which was Leicester Royal Infirmary. That was the hospital which effectively supported us at one of our lowest points when Janice was in there having a bone marrow transplant. Therefore, to be able to give something back to help others who may be in a situation like we were was wonderful. We had managed, after a year of trying, to find out who the best person to contact was to secure an initial meeting. Everything was going well until, five minutes from the hospital, I realised I had got the time wrong for the meeting and we should have been there an hour before. I was mortified.

By the time we arrived, rather than thinking we would only be fifteen minutes late, we were in fact one hour and fifteen minutes late. We were so angry at each other and blamed the other person for not checking. It was made worse by the fact we were already rushing; it was a hot day and because we would now have to rush around, we were both sweating and flustered. Not a good look. I seriously thought we had blown it.

They were luckily understanding and told us not to worry. They loved what we did and wanted our packs anyway. After that meeting, we both breathed a sigh of relief, the blame of getting the time wrong was swept under the carpet and it was now a moment to celebrate ticking off of a goal we wanted to achieve from the outset. It was the first time our charity work would be covering a city and such a large hospital, too. We made our first delivery to Leicester Royal Infirmary on 26 August 2018. We just hoped we would be able to keep up with the demands for the gifts once it started to take off.

The more we continued to give, the more the donations were flooding in. That was all good, but it meant that our house was being overtaken again and this time it was worse than before. The storeroom we had was full to the brim, dangerously full. This meant the overflow was our home.

We couldn't say no to the donations as we really did need them for the gift packs and they would help as it would save us money.

I remember the day a lorry came with boxes of Yorkshire Tea on pallets for one of our hot drink packs. He seemed confused as to why he was dropping them off at a house, and I had to convince him we weren't taking them to sell and I wasn't addicted to Yorkshire Tea. That was the final donation that tipped the house over the edge from being a house to a warehouse.

Even though we didn't let anyone know, we looked like a couple from those hoarder programmes you see on TV. Whilst we tried to make a joke of it, in reality, it actually wasn't funny. It made me feel anxious as I had no escapism, and I couldn't get comfortable. The only place I could get comfortable was to lie in my bed because that was the only place spared of clutter.

We knew we had to get another storeroom because, long-term, I couldn't live like this, so it was back to the storage centre in desperation to ask for more space. It meant we came away with a space around the size of two double-sized garages we could fill with items. It literally became a dumping ground because we didn't have time to get it organised into sections or categories. It was an absolute nightmare trying to find things. We spent more time looking for things to do our work than actually doing the work.

Before the end of the year, we won another two awards within three weeks of each other. Both completely unexpected, to be honest, and both a massive achievement for us. We never believed we were worthy enough to win because we were still pretty much trying to figure out how you do in fact run a charity.

At the time, no one really knew who we were unless you were in a hospital setting, and more often than not, you would get asked, "What is The Lewis Foundation?"

The first award was for SME Not for Profit of the Year in Northamptonshire. Lee and I went; we were a bag of nerves, and this meant we drank way too much to steady them. We were on a table who actually made us feel welcome, and we had a right laugh and drink with them. Therefore, even if we lost, I knew I would have had a good night out. When we won, we were over the moon.

The second award was the All Things Business Award that was going to be hosted by Jimmy Carr.

We loved him and hoped that we would get to meet him and have our photo with him, an opportunity we would only have if we won. This meant for us, the chances of that happening were pretty remote because we were up against some strong, well-known businesses.

Lee had been for an interview for this award, meeting the Chief of Northamptonshire Police. I asked Lee how it went; he said he couldn't remember a word other than that he told our story. This meant that he chatted his ear off. He either impressed him or talked him to death.

We had never had expectation or belief we would win. However, whatever Lee had said in that interview worked and we were genuinely shocked when he announced we had won; we looked at each other in amazement.

I prayed he wasn't going to rip us as he had done with everyone else. He didn't. Lee lost the ability to speak when he asked him questions, which was hilarious. Then we had our photo with him after and as I stood there, I couldn't believe what had just happened.

However, for us it was such a huge achievement because we received something that we never thought was possible and, more importantly, there was an understanding of the work we were doing. It did matter and it was important.

Christmas came and it was another year of hampers, this time reaching thirty-nine, and it was becoming easier to get nominations as people were starting to realise we were genuine. It continued to be a heart-warming and emotional experience, turning up at people's doors and surprising them. We also gave gifts to people in hospital who were going for day treatment too. We spent Christmas week going around the wards and cheering people up with gift boxes with a voucher and treats, before making our way around Talbot Butler Ward on Christmas Day.

The pace of the charity had really picked up that year. We had given away 12,900 gifts to adults going through treatment, which made us realise how busy we had been over the last year. The charity finally started to feel like it had taken off because people were finally understanding our mission and vision to help support people through cancer treatment.

2019

The pace of 2019 was unlike anything we could ever have imagined. We were wanted everywhere by everyone, which meant we were at everything. The hard graft over the last few years had well and truly kicked in and was starting to pay off.

The support we received was great. We had been asked to be 'Charity of the Year' by a number of businesses, donations were coming in and events were popping up all over the place, it was great. The hospitals were doing really well too. Packs were getting popular and gift handouts were going great. It was just really hard, and I wish I had had time to stop, take it in and enjoy it more, have a rest every now and again.

We felt we couldn't say no so accepted invitation after invitation. We showed up and we could always bring the energy to it, even on those mornings where one of us would be struggling and saying that we couldn't do it. We would kick each other up the bum to keep going and then crash after.

We made the decision that, with the rate it was going at the time and with everything going on, we couldn't do any more hospitals. We just needed to stay afloat with what we were already doing.

Both Lee and I were fully aware we needed to sort the charity and our personal life out because both were spiralling out of control. If a grip wasn't taken, it wasn't going to end in a good way.

We were both holding down full-time jobs, and there just didn't seem to be enough hours in the day to attend the events people wanted us at, fundraise, answer calls and respond to emails. So, it was all go from the minute we woke up until the minute our heads touched the pillow at night. This was seven days a week. There was no real time to eat properly or socialise, work out, have me time, have a relationship, maintain the house that was now completely wrecked. I was so tired.

I was a person that needed seven to eight hours sleep, and I was only getting three to four. I just felt wrecked. I had always had an iron deficiency but didn't have time to go to the doctor and sort it out. I found out I had fibroids, which also made me feel worse, yet I didn't make time to deal with it.

I didn't really see or do anything with Lee unless it was charity-related, and I missed just hanging out with my family and friends. If I had a pound for everyone I said 'sorry I can't make it' or 'I will need to come later' or to every time I had to cancel at the last minute because something had come up, I would be a millionaire.

The final straw for me, when something had to change, was when my mum told me she was struggling. I said, "Why didn't you tell me?" She said she didn't want to bother me as I was too busy. That really hurt me because my parents mean everything to me and to not know made me feel awful. The fact they could not tell me made me feel even worse.

I felt like I had lost control over my life and who I was. I made that choice to keep battling on, rather than to stop and do something about it. I was becoming physically and mentally drained in every aspect of my life. The momentum to keep going was requiring more and more effort.

People would say 'you look tired', but no one asked anything beyond that. So, it enabled me to keep this mask up that everything was fine. I could get away with saying 'I'm fine', when actually I felt anything but fine.

Lee knew I was struggling badly. I was feeling panicky and anxious, and he would see when I came home and saw the house filled from top to bottom with stuff, how it caused me to have panic attacks.

Lee took a month off work to try and help make things better, properly clearing out the house to give us some normality inside it again and sorting things that needed to be done to take the pressure off us both. We knew this was only a short-term solution as we knew as soon as he went back to work, it would start to build up again. However, if it helped make us feel better for the time being then so be it. It did for a little bit.

I didn't hate the charity; I still loved every aspect of it. I just needed a break. Yet, a break wasn't forthcoming, and I thought if I could ride it out until the two weeks I had off in September it would give me time to have a rest. I always booked time off in September. The weather was usually good; the kids were back to school so holiday prices would drop; and it was something to look forward to after the usual summer holiday period ended.

I had no plans for week one. I was going to try and rest and catch up on things with the charity that I hadn't had a chance to do, whilst throwing in some time for catch-ups. The following week, I was going to Ibiza. This was a trip I made annually following my sunset moment.

I genuinely believe there are moments, when things happen to help you when you are struggling. It was my thirty-fifth birthday, and I was out for lunch with my parents and brother when I got a call about something I had forgotten I even applied for: the Eden Project Nature in Leadership Retreat.

I had been selected and was told to come down for five days to take part in this retreat, which happened to be on the first week of my holiday, which I had no plans for other than to do charity work. I remember speaking to Pam from Eden on the phone, who said, "Even if you just come down for five days and rest, then you should take time out to do so." I had loads of things I needed to do and going away would put me five days behind. However, I thought about how I was feeling, and I decided that if I didn't take this, I would crumble as I could feel I was about to hit a wall.

As with all things Eden, there is never any agenda sent in advance; it was a wait and see. For someone who likes to know what is going on, that's really tough, and I was trying to work out whether I could fit in any work whilst I was there.

I remember packing up and driving down, as I would be staying on the Eden Project site. I hoped that I would get something that would help me to feel that little bit better, even if it was a week to catch up on some sleep.

I always feel calm when I'm there, and as soon as I stepped out of my car, that feeling came to me instantly. I knew by the end of the week I was going to feel so much better.

I remember on the first evening, we got to eat dinner in the biodome after hours. An incredible experience, let me tell you. Pam from Eden turned around and asked me where I wanted to take the charity. I said national without hesitation, which is something that I hadn't openly admitted before. When she asked how I was going to do that, the honest answer was that I had no clue but I knew in time it would happen. However, before I could even think about that, I needed to get my life together.

That week changed everything for me. It was a week that actually saved me. I was with such an incredible and supportive group of people. Despite the fact I had never met them before, we were able to open up to each other and trust each other.

For the first time, I was able to share how much I was struggling, how I really felt. I cried a lot, the only time I felt safe to, and no one judged me for being weak or a weirdo. Listening to others, what they were going through and what they were trying to achieve also made me feel less alone.

As the week moved on, every day I felt lighter, a little bit better, I had a clearer plan of action and felt more like me again.

I never had time to work that week; I never really had access to my mobile and the sun shone all week, so we pretty much spent the majority of the time outdoors. Being in nature and the sunshine always makes me feel so good. At the end of that week, I felt like a whole new person, ready to get back out there, and I knew that I had to make changes.

The final thing we did was write a scroll with our plans on it, starting with where we wanted to be in the future, working our way back to where we are now. So, I had a focus, a plan of action to work towards rather than drifting.

It was a retreat that probably saved me from long-term burnout, health issues, breakdown, heartache – potentially a combo of all of them. They threw me a lifeline that I will forever be grateful for.

That day I left the Eden Project, it took me nine hours to get home because of an accident on the motorway. But I didn't care; everything felt different. I felt lighter. Like a weight had lifted off my shoulders. I was so excited to go away the next afternoon.

The next day I did a hospital visit at lunchtime around Talbot Butler Ward giving out gifts, before flying to Ibiza in the afternoon. A week of rest, sleep and just being me again. I never slept so much or rested so much in my life. But the sunshine, good company and some time out was just what I needed.

When I came home, I was able to sort things out. I knew I had to put me first and everything else would flow from that. I got myself booked into the doctors and sorted out my health so I could start to feel better.

I realised that to keep the charity afloat, it meant asking for help. It was really hard to do that for us as we didn't want to bother people or put anyone out. We were also conscious of the fact that the chaos of our life meant that the charity was unorganised, which had always made it hard to get others involved in helping. We realised there would be no us if we didn't take this step; as hard it was, it was the right thing to do.

We spent the next few months doing that and I started to feel more in control; we were starting to feel better. The year ended with so much positivity and I felt that, after all that darkness, I could finally see the light.

The month of December brought a number of good pieces of news which, after the rest of the year's struggles, was the boost that we really needed.

We were contacted by Luton & Dunstable Hospital and asked to provide our packs there. We hadn't taken on a hospital for nearly a year, but we felt ready to. It was such a good feeling to make our delivery there, knowing that we would be helping even more people. They were excited as much as we were, which always filled us with so much joy. A new hospital, another chapter and a greater opportunity to make a difference.

It was that time of year when we were ready to start our Christmas hamper giving in the community. I had just started to use LinkedIn as a place where I could network with the business community and share what we do. I started to share what we were doing and one evening I decided to share a post about our Christmas hampers.

Ann sent me a DM asking if she could help and use her network to also help us. She was able to get wonderful members of the community to help not only sponsor the hampers but also make them. We cannot tell you how grateful we were for that true act of kindness because usually we would have tried to do this all on our own, which normally made the month of December relentless. It enabled us to then just focus on the Christmas hamper delivery. This year, we split into groups for the delivery of the hampers so we could take our time with the handouts and give people time, like we wanted. It was fun and we loved every minute of it.

We also received an invitation to the Queen's Royal Garden Party the following year. When I received the invite I was absolutely shocked, and I couldn't believe it. Lee's reaction was the same when I told him.

It was for May next year and I couldn't wait to have a potential opportunity to meet the Queen – that would make my day, week, year and beyond. I have no clue who nominated us for this invite, but I will be forever grateful to them because we were touched someone thought that much of us to put us forward.

The year ended with a big surprise when we were contacted to say that Lee and I were going to receive a British Citizen Award. We had been nominated to receive an award and a medal at the Palace of Westminster for our work founding The Lewis Foundation. We would even have letters after our names. A national honour. We were so shocked, genuinely shocked. We never set out to do this for any recognition or reward. It amazed us that they thought we were deserving enough to receive it.

We thought we could try and keep it low profile as we don't like to make a fuss. We got that totally wrong as the British Citizen Award had contacted our local paper, and we were getting messages of congratulations about it. That was even before we had shared it with anyone. The messages were incredible, the support, the stories people were sharing of how they received a gift. We were totally blown away. Our local newspaper, *Chronicle & Echo*, put us on the front page, which I had no clue about until we kept getting tagged in pictures of it.

It was a huge deal for people, and it was to us. Never when we started did we even dream of something like this happening.

Christmas Day came in a blink of an eye. We had raised enough money separately doing a Christmas appeal to enable us to go into hospital on Christmas morning to provide gifts to cancer patients at Northampton General Hospital. It was a mixture of hampers, gift boxes and vouchers going to the patients. There were also gifts for the staff working that shift too. It was a really great morning. A great way to start Christmas before going to do your own thing with your family.

That year, we had given away 24,800 gifts. A huge achievement for us. We were ending the year feeling slightly more organised, a bit more in control and also having learnt a lesson about the importance of self-care. It was a new decade, which we felt would be an exciting one.

2020

The year started off great, with lots of businesses coming forward asking us to be their Charity of the Year. People were letting us know about fundraising events they'd planned. We were planning to host our own fundraiser: Lap of Honour. A walking lap to help remember, support and thank people going through cancer treatment. It was going to be a good year.

Our packs were continuing to go to the hospitals and the numbers were going up, which was great, due to word of mouth.

It felt like we were on the right path.

We started the year off on a high, going to receive our British Citizen Award in January. Both of our mums were able to go, something they were both excited about. We were so nervous as we checked into the queue to go through security at the Houses of Parliament, not sure what to expect. There were so many people there all dressed up and ready to receive their awards. We sat there listening as Michael Underwood read out and introduced each person and it just felt surreal as I was looking around the room. A room full of the most amazing people. Then he read out about us and called us up, and we received our medals.

Following the ceremony, we did an open-top lap of honour on a bus around London, which was amazing even if we nearly froze to death driving around London. That still didn't stop us lapping it up and making sure we took our selfies.

It then ended with another ceremony where we were presented with our certificates and, this time, Michael Underwood asked us questions about our charity work to share with the audience.

It was an absolutely incredible day and one I will remember forever.

Receiving this British Citizen Award had really boosted our level of support and awareness for the work we do.

The charity was starting to get that busy feeling again, and I just prayed it wouldn't get to the stage where it got to the time before – that runaway train feeling. I didn't want to go back down that path again.

We were contacted by Nottingham Hospital, who reached out to see if we could support their patients, having seen our work at Leicester Royal Infirmary. A meeting was scheduled for March to see how we could get set up and make it happen. This was really exciting to head somewhere new.

However, at the beginning of March 2020, things started to change; the start of the month was really weird. There were talks of the virus, but it shouldn't impact us as, by the looks of it, it was far overseas. Everyone was really dismissive. I was completely dismissive of it. "It's not going to affect us, and how can it be that serious?" How naïve was I?

However, I was driving home from work on 11 March. It was a Friday, which meant our weekly evening gift hand out would happen in a couple of hours. Lee called me and said, "I don't think we can get into the hospital anymore. Everyone is being really weird and cautious due to the virus."

I said, "It can't be that bad." I told him he was being stupid, that it wasn't that bad. Yet, Lee was adamant. He said when doing a hospital visit earlier that day everyone was really nervous to be approached or take anything. Something which we had never experienced before. Then a member of staff from another hospital messaged me saying it was bad and you should pause the charity for a while to protect the patients and yourself. I knew then that it really was bad. Yet, I didn't want to hear it or accept the truth because I knew that accepting it meant that we would have to stop The Lewis Foundation. Stop the thing that we had been doing for the last four years.

We didn't really want to stop, but what choice did we have when the hospitals were saying this was going to get really bad? Our work meant the people we were supporting were classed as vulnerable. We didn't want to put anyone at risk. As painful as it was for us to stop, people came first, and with that, it meant pausing our services.

We genuinely believed at the time that it was something that would blow over in a matter of weeks, maybe a couple of months at a push.

I was so upset as I typed the message that we were going to pause and pressed send online. A part of me just felt empty, like what do I do now? For the first time in four years, what was I going to do outside my day job?

People were really understanding. They knew we hated it, but it was the right thing to do. Despite everyone's understanding and support, it didn't make us feel any better.

We were one of the first people I saw who decided to stop. We thought, *why is no one else?* Maybe we had made a mistake and been over the top. However, slowly messages were appearing from other organisations who were saying they were going to have to stop too. That's when it really hit home and felt scary because no one had a clue what was going on. You had no one to turn to for guidance or support.

Then there was the moment, the announcement on 23 March 2020, when everything changed. We remember sitting down in shock. Sitting there listening to what Boris Johnson was saying. We couldn't believe what we were hearing. It didn't sound real. It couldn't possibly be real. All these restrictions. Only leaving your house once a day, not being able to see your family in person, all the businesses being forced to close, schools closing – the list went on. Like a disaster film, except this time we were the characters.

The aim was to live this way for twelve weeks, three months. OK, we could do that, but mentally I wasn't OK.

I felt constantly worried about everyone, in particular my parents, who I checked on constantly via phone calls to make sure they were healthy. With Lee working in the care home, I thought he was going to get the virus and it would kill him. I thought I was going to get it too and the same would happen to me. I just felt panicky constantly. We worried about the people we supported who were vulnerable, what would happen to them and how they would cope. I didn't sleep, which made me feel even worse about everything that was going on. I was exhausted and a bag of nerves.

I felt a complete loss of control over my own life. For the first time, Lee and I were forced to do nothing but spend time together. Time not doing charity-related stuff but actual time together. Not that we could do much, but we could be together; we could learn to discover who we were as Lorraine and Lee again.

This period was an opportunity for us to rest and recharge, which we needed. Even though it felt totally weird to do.

The weather was so good; we lived in the garden; we ate and drank far too much. I slowly learnt to quieten my mind so I could sleep by doing yoga and morning/evening meditation.

After nearly two months of living like this, some of the hospitals were getting in contact asking where we were and if we could bring in some packs. We were surprised, as we didn't even think continuing was an option. However, they said it would help. Visiting had been restricted, and it would help to put people at ease and feel a little bit better. So, if we could find a way, please could we continue.

The two of us sat there and planned how we could make this work because all the ways we used to make this happen were blocked. We had no access to the shops as only essential shops were open; we couldn't meet with our volunteers; the centre we used to pack in was closed; and how were we even going to hand them out? We knew we had to adapt everything, and with no guidebook to go to, it was going to have to be a mixture of trial and error and seeing what happened.

We fully underestimated how hard it was going to be to get the gift items in the first place. The shelves were stripped of everything. To the point where, when you can't even get things like underwear, you really do realise that people are just panic buying because who stocks up on underwear? The whole experience of trying to go into a supermarket and local wholesalers – the only place that was open to get what we needed, seeing people desperate out of fear – was terrifying. The empty shelves freaked me out and I kept thinking I was going to get ill. Every time I went in the shops, I felt like I couldn't breathe as I couldn't comprehend what was going on.

Realising this option wasn't going to work, the only hope we had was to contact places directly and pray they would help us. We reached out to the shops and wholesalers we used. Knowing we genuinely needed the items, they saved them for us, even having to disguise them, especially the hand sanitisers which became as valuable as gold. They gave us what they could for free, but when we did have to purchase things, the prices had risen so ridiculously high.

It was a scary time, scary in that we didn't know long-term what we were going to do in relation to funding and income. Scary in that we were learning as we went and adapting to ensure we could continue what we were doing safely. We didn't initially know how to sort gift packing with the volunteers, seeing as we were packing in our community centre before that. The centre was shut and now it was game over due to social distancing.

At first, Janice, who was in isolation, would pack the gifts for the hospital – all of them – and that was a crazy job in itself. However, we really didn't know how else to do it, and it was the safest place as she had been in lockdown before lockdown even started.

Then, the storeroom where we stored all our items turned around and said, "We may have to close, so you might want to get out what you really need as it could close overnight." Now our storeroom was full, and we knew we couldn't take everything. So, we had to select what was key and split it between our house and Janice's house. We went back to the days when our house was overtaken, a temporary warehouse, but what else could we do?

We had agreed with the hospitals that we would drop our gifts off, and they would facilitate the handouts, so we didn't have to worry about putting ourselves or the patients at risk.

When the hospital was seen as a coronavirus-filled building, I was absolutely terrified about going into that setting, even to drop the packs off. Yet, I had to put that fear aside to just get on with what needed to be done, and as long as I took measures to protect myself, that would give me some reassurance.

The process allowed us to support from a distance, not in the way we liked, but at least we were helping. This enabled us to get back up off the ground and continue, and the messages coming back from patients and hospital staff showed we were helping. This gave us both the drive and push to keep going and also helped to take our mind off what was going on around us by having a focus.

People saw we were continuing and were continually reaching out to support us. Big businesses such as Tesco, Aviva, Waitrose and more. Members of the community were reaching out to support us too. Everyone wanted to play a part in helping to feel like they were doing something to help in a situation where we all felt completely helpless. That level of kindness and support surprised me as we had never experienced or seen anything like that before. Everyone came together in a time when there was so much pain.

For the people who were shielding that we would normally support, it was an absolutely horrific time, being told not to leave their house at all. If you were on your own, you were completely disconnected and isolated from the world. The people who were shielding, their family and friends were reaching out to ask if we could help get things to them.

We then started to hand out packs to people in the community. Basic things such as toilet roll, cleaning products and toiletries that were scarce or things to occupy the mind such as magazines, puzzle books etc.

We would then deliver them to people's homes with our volunteers. It was weird not having any contact with people, just dropping and going as we were terrified of making anyone ill. It was weird seeing people and not being our usual selves – handshakes/hugs – and keeping our distance. It just felt so unnatural to us.

The more we continued to give, the greater support and coverage we got. We were mentioned in *The Sun*, which we couldn't believe. A small feature about what we were doing during lockdown but enough to get people's attention about our work, which was encouraging more people to donate.

We decided to give gifts to the hospital staff to support them. They were working around the clock dealing with a virus that no one had ever dealt with before. We brought them gift packages to treat them too. Pamper bags, food treats, whatever we could do to boost them. Those people were true heroes who worked their socks off without complaint to save the lives of others and be family members to patients, whose actual family couldn't be there.

What was wonderful to see were the floods of donations pouring in from businesses for the hospital staff and patients – everything and anything. Food, hot meals, toiletries, magazines etc. I remember walking into

Kettering General Hospital to drop something off and a whole hall had been transformed to deal with donations. It was actually great to see the NHS staff, care workers, supermarket workers and anyone in a public-facing job getting the respect and recognition they'd always deserved. Still showing up to work and doing their job despite the risk to their health.

For us, the charity was continuing to operate and that was an amazing achievement. However, whilst the packs continued to go out, not as much money was coming in. We had been drastically hit as a result of fundraising opportunities being lost. Every fundraising event had been cancelled and that was our main source of income.

It was getting concerning that the virus was lingering on longer than originally anticipated, which meant every month we were losing out financially. I was terrified that, long-term, we would have to stop completely because we had run out of money.

I saw that the lottery was doing a COVID-19 fund and decided to apply for support for the gifts and support Lee in getting a wage. Lee was doing a night shift and trying to still do charity work at the same time, which was becoming virtually impossible, and he was wrecked. Often, he would finish a night shift and then go on to do charity work, meaning he wasn't even having a chance to rest. I could do no more to help him as I was working too, and it was relentless as we tried to adapt to a new way of working. I applied for £32,000 with no belief that we would get it.

I never imagined we would get it, no way. We had been refused before the pandemic. Then we had a message saying to call back, the lottery has some good news.

I couldn't accept that we had got this funding until I heard the words directly. I was genuinely shocked, but in this dark time, it was the best news I ever could have heard. It was just like a wave of relief had washed over me. Relief from the financial worry and, more importantly, Lee's health in that he wouldn't have to work in the way he had been.

£32,000 that would keep us going whilst we figured out alternative ways to bring in money.

Lee could now work for the charity in a part-time capacity. We had never ever had an intention for paid roles within the charity when we started. However, with the size of the charity, the only way for us to enable it to continue and to make it work long-term was for this to happen. After this other funding we applied for started to come in.

If it wasn't for funding support and people doing virtual fundraisers for us, I literally don't know where we would be or how long we could have continued. We saw so many other charities around us stop forever. Who would look after them now, who would be there for these people?

We were so grateful that in times like this, we were able to keep going due to people helping us.

Every week through lockdown, Janice continued to pack the gifts and we delivered them. People were in hospital alone, no network or support around them. I couldn't even begin to imagine how hard that must have been, not having any contact, and the packs were helping to lift people's spirits even though we couldn't physically be there in person.

We had some great things happen to boost awareness of our cause nationally. We were featured in *HELLO!* magazine's #HelloToKindness – being on a page amongst celebrities was pretty unreal. We also made *The Independent* newspaper's

Happy List 2020 for COVID-19 heroes – it was pretty awesome to make the same list as Captain Sir Tom.

The biggest shock of all came one night when we received an email to say we had received a Points of Light Award from Boris Johnson. I read the email and was debating whether it was fake. There was a phone number to call if you wanted to check.

I shared this email with Lee, who said it seemed a bit dodgy. I spoke to my parents, and they're super cautious, and they agreed it seemed dodgy.

Being in two minds, I decided to make contact the next day and it was confirmed it was real. They'd heard about our work from *The Independent* newspaper. To be recognised in this way for our work during the pandemic, especially by someone of this level, it really meant a lot to us. It motivated us to keep going forward and that we were doing something positive during a really scary time. We were sent a signed certificate and letter too. We can't tell you how proud we were to receive it.

So much had happened over the summer months and it finally seemed like things were starting to get better – restrictions were slowly lifting, and it looked like we would be getting back to some type of normality. Social distancing was still in place which meant we couldn't use our local community centre.

Our volunteers wanted to get involved again and we were determined that this was something that was really important to people. We figured out a plan and got the volunteers involved in our gift packing again but this time from home, which overcame the issue of social distancing.

We already isolated every gift item that came in. We then left them for a few days before we dropped them off at people's homes. They would pack and then isolate the tubs for a few days. We would collect them, isolate them again before they made their way to the hospital. So, the turnaround time was significantly longer but if we kept on top of it, we could ensure a continuing flow of gifts went to patients in hospital. Once we got into a routine, we were still able to get a continuous supply of packs going out each week.

Once restrictions lifted, we started at Nottingham City Hospital and Queens Medical Centre in August 2020. After months of planning and delays caused due to COVID-19, we could finally make it happen. They were as excited as we were. We were late as we got lost – no surprise there! However, they were blown away by the number of gifts: over a thousand with the first delivery – it was incredible. The hospitals were huge, so many wards in comparison to the hospitals we were currently dealing with.

During that summer, we realised we needed further help and support with not only fundraising but also the organisational things behind the scenes: organising the storeroom, sorting out the stock and donations, getting generally organised so we knew what the hell was happening. We had an amazing volunteer called Lynette who was helping where she could with this. She had received our packs in hospital, one of our hampers, and was going above and beyond to help us in the background. We knew Lynette was someone who got why we did what we did and was passionate about helping as much as we were – she was the best person for the job. We were so glad when she said yes to joining our team, as we knew she would help make such a wonderful difference to our charity and it was a positive step forward for us to do an even better job. From day one she made a difference.

By the end of summer, we were on a high and thought we were over the worst.

We wished things could have stayed that way, on the up, the virus ending instead of seeming to get worse again. When we were planning for the future and hoping for the best, never did we imagine another lockdown would happen. I was scared. Lee was so positive, but I was just worried, especially income-wise. Charities never got any government funding, yet they were directly helping support society – it just felt so unfair.

We applied for another lottery fund to help get us through this next period but were refused, which I can understand. We already had one and there were so many causes out there who had needs greater than ours.

I just didn't know what to do to get through another period of uncertainty. We had wanted to do an event called Lap of Honour. This would be a fundraising event where everyone would come together to do a lap of our local park to support, thank or remember someone. However, the restrictions meant we could not do this. We decided to press ahead with our Lap of Honour fundraiser virtually. We knew it wasn't going to be the same, but we thought, *let's do it anyway*. We had some amazing people act as ambassadors and take part.

We raised £3,378, more than we thought possible, and having never done any fundraising of this scale before, that sum of money was a huge deal to us and it would help go towards supporting costs for a month. Yet for me, the sleepless nights crept back in and the constant worry about whether we would be able to continue wouldn't go away.

However, because of that Lap of Honour, something really special happened. It's in these moments throughout the charity when we have these worries or struggles that someone always comes to save us.

I had an email come through with a letter regarding a substantial donation that someone wished to make to our charity. Again, I thought it was dodgy. We had been getting constantly blasted with random emails offering large sums of money that were clearly fake. However, I did some online stalking and the donor seemed legitimate. Yet I still didn't believe it. I called the number and said I had received this email, and I wasn't entirely sure they were genuine. Yes, I said that. She laughed and said she could understand that, but it wasn't a fake email, and the donation was real, all £53,000 of it. I then burst into tears on the phone. I cried down the phone as she was speaking to me, trying to convey my gratitude at how much this meant. How much this was going to save us and get us through the pandemic. I literally couldn't stop crying. I remember getting off the phone and telling Lee who couldn't believe this was true either, before saying, "You didn't cry down the phone, did you?"

All that worry and stress melted away in that one phone call. We could help people; we could survive this pandemic without worrying. It just made me realise the power of social media. You never know who is silently watching what you're doing.

The money came a week later, and everything just felt so much safer. We could relax and get back to what we loved to do. I will be forever grateful for that donation and the wonderful anonymous donor that came forward to make it possible.

It was coming up to Christmas and we wanted to do the Christmas hamper surprise again. This year, we knew it would be socially distanced, but we were still intent on doing it. We put out an appeal for sponsors and were so grateful to the people who came forward, individuals and businesses wanting to donate to support someone and make this possible. We knew this year was tough and didn't expect a great level of support. However, the level of support we received was greater than we could ever have imagined.

We had applied for funding from two funders – Northamptonshire Community Foundation and Milton Keynes Community Foundation – and were so happy to learn we were successful with both. Then, people were responding to our appeal for sponsors for the hampers too. Our original plan was to give out thirty hampers. We got so much support, the total leapt to 121, the most we had ever given. Above that, we were having companies host gift drives for presents, people donating gifts and fundraising – it was amazing.

We were so keen to support local businesses as much as we could, putting out an appeal to work with them and purchasing the items for the hampers from local businesses. Our volunteers helped out with the packing of the hampers from their homes and Metro Bank in Northampton got their staff involved in packaging hampers.

This time, to inject some additional festive cheer, I dressed up in whatever outfit I could find. Elf, Christmas Tree and Christmas Pudding were some that I wore during that gift giving. I love fancy dress anyway, so it was right up my street. Lee stuck with a Christmas hat; he is not as much into fancy dress as I am. Even though it was socially distanced, it was so uplifting and moving, coordinating with families to give the surprise gift, with the help of our amazing PA Marlen. We saw happy tears, shock, disbelief – all positive reactions to strangers making this possible to make them feel better. It really moved us as much as it did the recipients.

This year, to help us with the handouts, the hospitals got involved, with us asking them to pick patients they knew who should receive a hamper from our charity. They also helped hand them out too, which brought so much joy to the nurses doing it. The feedback we got from them and the recipients was amazing.

I was buzzing as it was leading up to Christmas week and I was really looking forward to it, to actually get to spend some time with my family over the five-day period. All this hard work was gearing up to that. We were going away just locally to have a break as we hadn't stopped since the pandemic started. So, we would see our family and do this too.

Then the announcement came that the rules had changed, and it was only Christmas Day that we could see your family. This meant because I was away, I wouldn't see my family. Whilst I totally got that it had to change, it didn't mean I couldn't feel upset, angry and disappointed.

I just felt gutted and flat for days after. I felt like giving up; this virus was doing me in. Lee and I were driving each other forward to keep going as the news knocked the wind out of us. If it wasn't for the final set of hampers to lift our spirits, I would have just locked myself away in my house. However, we finished the last hamper on 23 December. Then we did our final drop off of Christmas Day gifts on Christmas Eve to Talbot Butler Ward. We were gutted we weren't going to get to do Christmas Day, but circumstances were different this year with the virus. The nurses would hand them out on Christmas morning for us instead.

Following a doorstep visit to see my family on Christmas Eve, we checked into Fawsley Hall hotel Christmas Eve afternoon. The guests cut right back as Northamptonshire by some miracle were still in tier two, which meant as we checked in on Christmas Eve, we could stay there over Christmas. However, we needed that break to rest finally after one of the craziest years since we began. We made it and just hoped that 2021 would be better. It had to be better. It couldn't be any worse than this.

However, we were proud of what we achieved. We still managed to get out 21,167 gifts. We still managed to somehow make the charity work, thanks to our community, and that was nothing short of incredible. They were always there for us and believing in what we were trying to achieve and what we were trying to do. We decided for the first time in a long time to take some time out and rest.

As we sat there on 31 December 2020, the strangest New Year's Eve ever due to having to remain indoors, we reflected on the year and charity in general. We couldn't believe we had made it. We knew how fortunate we were to still be here and surviving, as we had seen many be hit financially really hard and some had to close. We felt sad with the number of people we had known that had died that year through COVID-19 or due to cancer; it was a painful fact that we never even had the opportunity to see them or say goodbye.

2021 had to be better; it couldn't be worse than this. With talks of the vaccine, it sounded more positive, and it would get better. We were determined we would still be there on the other side of the virus and that we would continue to help as many people as possible until that day arrived.

2021

2021 for us started with negative news of another national lockdown. For me, it was just too much. It had now been going on for far too long. It was winter; it was dark; it was cold, and we still couldn't do the charity in the way we would have liked to do it. I just felt really low and stuck in a rut. I think it was during this lockdown out of all of them when I finally had enough.

We tried to map out our plans for 2021, but how do you map out plans when you don't know what is going on from one minute to the next? It was just so hard to work out what to do and how we were going to keep surviving through this. So many organisations were either making serious cutbacks or were closing their doors and saying they could no longer continue. We didn't want that to be us, which meant we would do whatever we could to keep going. Thankfully, due to people stepping forward to fundraise, and that large donation in November, we would be fine for now. I just worried for how long. It was great to have Lee at my side reassuring me, keeping me positive and helping to push my mindset past doom and gloom.

That month, we were contacted by both Chesterfield Royal Hospital and Lincolnshire Hospitals who had heard of the impact of our work and wanted our packs to help support patients through their treatment and whilst in hospital. We had meetings with both hospitals who were as excited as we were to get this started. We were nervous too. What if it failed? What if we ran out of money? Were we taking on too much? However, it was the right thing to do, and we knew we would make things work, so we went for it. It gave me something positive to focus on, knowing we could help even more people.

We launched at these hospitals within a week of each other at the beginning of February. It meant it really pushed our reach around the Midlands of where we provided our support. People were concerned for us that we were taking on too much. Trusting our gut instinct, sometimes you had to take risks, and if we hadn't, I know for a fact we would have regretted it.

Also, COVID-19 had got us to a point where for the first time we had sorted out all the items in the background, and that meant we were organised. This meant for us we were not under immense pressure like we had been in previous years and felt so good to operate in this way.

By partnering with these hospitals, we were now supporting fourteen NHS hospitals around the Midlands. We had doubled the size of support during the pandemic. We knew this was simply the beginning of our work and as we moved out of lockdown, and hopefully back to normal life, we were excited to see where our charity would take us next and what else The Lewis Foundation would achieve.

* * *

I can't wait until social distancing ends so we can get back out into the community, doing our face-to-face work and spending time with patients. This was the thing we loved the most and this was at the heart of what we did when the charity began.

With the vaccines taking place and things starting to seem like they're getting better, life definitely looks better than it did a year ago. We had been able to keep going through the worst times possible, and that meant that we had been able to make our fifth birthday. Who would have believed it? We made five years!

On 7 April, not being able to celebrate in the way we liked, the two of us sat and raised a glass of champagne to toast what had been achieved. What a journey we had been on.

I still to this day don't know what our long-term plan was when we created the charity. Our idea had been born out of a period of sadness, loss and pain, and I believe a desperation to help lessen the suffering of others. The charity has evolved over the years into something that I'm so incredibly proud of. A beautiful light in a period of darkness. We created something that we never could have imagined would help bring together so many people. It taught me so much about myself, my life and that I was capable of more than I thought possible. I have met and connected with so many people who have enriched my life in a way I could never have imagined. You learn a lot about life when you sit with people who don't know whether they're going to live, and their time is running out. That made me appreciate my life and gave me a sense of gratitude for what I have and how I live. It changed me from a materialistic person to one who values people and experiences over things. All this overall has made me a stronger and better person.

It has given me a better perception of society and community, that people want to come together and that strangers will help each other out. I didn't believe that existed at all, but it clearly does, as I have witnessed this every day for the last five years. So many people have helped us on the path of our journey, and without them we wouldn't exist. Some people we have never even met, but the impact of our work meant so much they had to do something.

So where do we go next? We're still continuing to grow, with more hospitals in the pipeline. We have plans to develop our 'pamper days' and run them more frequently and get a place of our own so we can involve the community in the work of our charity.

Not one of us knows when we'll face cancer, whether it's ourselves or someone we love. We hope that our charity will inspire others with our mission not to let people go through this alone.

To many more years of continuing to spread the love via The Lewis Foundation.

AUTHOR'S BIOGRAPHY

Lorraine Lewis, together with her husband Lee Lewis, co-founded multi-award-winning cancer charity The Lewis Foundation, which provides free gifts and support to adult cancer patients in fourteen hospitals around the Midlands. The charity also extends this service into the community via 'The Lewis Foundation Pamper Days', which are a series of events throughout the year enabling patients to take time out for themselves to learn tools and techniques to address their physical and mental well-being.

Lorraine is also a lawyer, working for Crown Prosecution Service. This is a role Lorraine balances around her charity work.

Since starting The Lewis Foundation in 2016, Lorraine has regularly delivered motivational talks to school children, universities and businesses, such as the Eden Project, RCI Europe, Kindfest and De Montfort University Global Alumni. Lorraine has also featured in the media such as *The Sun*, *Hello!* and *Channel 4 News* talking about the journey of The Lewis Foundation to become the charity it is today.

In 2020, Lorraine received the prime minister's Point of Light Award, British Citizen Award and was named on *The*

Independent newspaper's Happy List 2020. Lorraine recently won *Hello!* Magazine Hello to Kindness for her positive impact in supporting cancer patients through their cancer journey.

ACKNOWLEDGEMENTS

I wouldn't be where I am today without the unwavering support of the two most incredible people in my life: my mum and dad. I really don't know what I would have done without you both. You were always there for me, always believed in me and never let anyone stop me achieving my dreams. I love you both so much and without you I wouldn't be where I am today, living the life of my dreams. I'm so lucky to have you both – thank you for everything you have done and continue to do for me.

Thank you to Lee who has been the most incredible source of support to me since you came into my life aged twenty. You were always there for me, supported me and put up with me as I pursued my legal dream. You encouraged me to keep going and do my best. Now we have created something really special after a period of so much pain together. It hasn't always been easy but look at what we have achieved. I can't imagine taking on this journey with anyone else.

Thank you to Janice and Chris, my mother- and father-in-law. From day one, you always supported my dreams as

I tried to qualify to become a barrister. You showed greater support to me than even my family did and would always be there if I needed anything.

Janice, you showed so much strength during your cancer journey and your grief, something that I have so much admiration for. I'm so grateful for all you do to continue to support us and help us get the charity to where it is today.

To Chris, wherever you are. I wish you were here to be involved in our journey, but I know you're supporting and cheering us along. You were one of the kindest and most giving person I have ever met, who would do anything for anyone, no matter what. Thank you for showing me the true meaning of kindness.